ON TRACK INVESTING

ON TRACK INVESTING

A Guide To Simulation Trading

DAVID R. HEBERT

Lighthouse Publishing Group, Inc.
Seattle, Washington

Lighthouse Publishing Group, Inc.
Copyright © 1999 David R. Hebert

Library of Congress Cataloging-in-Publication Data

Hebert, David R., 1942-
  On track investing : a guide to simulation trading/David R. Hebert
    p. cm.
  ISBN 0-910019-79-7
  1. Electronic trading of securities--Simulation methods.
I. Title. II. Title: Guide to simulation trading.
HG4515.95.H43 1998
332.64'2'0285--DC21
                           98-27600
                             CIP

Source Code: OTI98

"This publication is designed to provide accurate and authoritative information in regard to the subject matter covered. It is sold with the understanding that the publisher is not engaged in rendering legal, accounting, or other professional service. If legal or other expert assistance is required, the services of a competent professional person should be sought."

From a declaration of principles jointly adopted by a committee of the American Bar Association and a committee of the Publisher's Association.

Lighthouse Publishing Group, Inc. would like to thank the following people for their invaluable help, without which *On Track Investing* would not be possible:

Executive Director: Jerald Miller
Production Director: Brent Magarrell
Promotion Director: K. Noel Thomas
Book Design: Judy Burkhalter
Dust Jacket Design: Cynthia Fliege
Editing and Proofing: Barry L. Pyeatt, Grace Liu McLinn, Sam Hemenway,
  and David McKinlay.

Published by Lighthouse Publishing Group, Inc.
14675 Interurban Avenue South
Seattle, Washington 98168-4664
1-800-706-8657
(206) 901-3100 (fax)
www.lighthousebooks.com

Printed in the United States of America
10 9 8 7 6 5 4 3 2 1

To my wife, Diana,
who has stuck with me these past 36 years and made me what I am.
And to all of my children, their spouses, and my grandchildren.

CONTENTS

THE RESOURCES

Other Books By
Lighthouse Publishing Group, Inc.

Wealth 101, Wade Cook

Brilliant Deductions, Wade Cook

The Secret Millionaire Guide to Nevada Corporations
John V. Childers, Jr.

Million Heirs, John V. Childers, Jr.

Bear Market Baloney, Wade Cook

Blueprints for Success, Volume 1, Various Authors

Rolling Stocks, Gregory Witt

Sleeping Like A Baby, John Hudelson

Stock Market Miracles, Wade Cook

Wall Street Money Machine, Wade Cook

101 Ways To Buy Real Estate Without Cash, Wade Cook

Cook's Book On Creative Real Estate, Wade Cook

How To Pick Up Foreclosures, Wade Cook

Owner Financing, Wade Cook

Real Estate Money Machine, Wade Cook

Real Estate For Real People, Wade Cook

A+, Wade Cook

Business Buy The Bible, Wade Cook

Don't Set Goals, Wade Cook

Wade Cook's Power Quotes, Volume 1, Wade Cook

Y2K Gold Rush, Wade Cook

Living In Color, Renae Knapp

FOREWORD

In my books and seminars, I often tell about an important lesson taught to me many years ago. You often hear people say, "Practice makes Perfect." But that's wrong! It's only a half-truth. Only perfect practice makes perfect. If you practice something incorrectly, you will never learn to do it perfectly.

That's why I was so excited when I found out that David was writing this book. It's the perfect companion to help beginning investors practice perfectly.

Before any investor risks their hard-earned cash in the market, it's important to spend time not just practicing, but practicing in a careful consistent way.

Over the course of the last 30 years, I've had many opportunities to work closely with David. He is a seasoned, professional investor, but he, like many of us, has the financial battle scars to prove it. He has brought together years of experience, combined with exhaustive research into *On Track Investing*. The result is a fast-paced, thorough, guided tour of how you can learn to make big returns without risking your hard-earned cash.

He presents exactly how anyone, who has the desire, interest, and persistence can apply some of the most high-powered strategies for maximum profit potential. But he not only gives the basic strategies every investor needs to know, he also outlines exactly how to do the basics. He shows you how to develop a game plan, teaches you the basics of charting, and then tells you how to put that information to use.

But he also takes the next crucial step in teaching effectively. He helps you to practice, practice, practice (but practice perfectly).

You now have in your hands the knowledge and strategies which can give you the potential to not only change lives, but to affect fortunes, family dynasties, retirements, and financial destinies.

Once you have positioned yourself mentally for financial success, then the proven strategies, formulas, and patterns that are revealed in this book, combined with the tools to practice them perfectly, can help you make it a reality. Don't settle for anything less.

Wade B. Cook
New York Times Best-Selling Author,
Wall Street Money Machine
Stock Market Miracles

PREFACE

Simutrading is a tool.
If used by a competent hand,
It can produce beautiful,
Intricate results.
If used by a fool,
All is folly.
Most fall in between.

This is a basic instruction book for the tool of investing which does not require you to risk any money—paper trading. The system presented here is entitled Simutrading—a simulation of real trading. Glean what you can and then start a diligent practice. Be honest. Be accurate.

Simutrading is not an end unto itself. I have yet to meet a person who became wealthy by Simutrading alone. It is a tool to teach and learn. It is a tool to practice the skills of investing and decision making. It can be used as an evaluation tool to see if a specific strategy is having the results that you desire. If deficiency pops up its head, then Simutrading can be the tool to fine tune. The "game," either Simutrade or cash, can be tracked by your bottom line. Therefore, although Simutrading is not an end unto itself, it does have an end—real, cash trades with profitable results.

As with all tools, it is just that, a tool. It doesn't actually make anything by itself, but it is essential when specialized help is needed. Simutrading's best benefit is intangible. It's the knowledge, synaptic response (skill), and habit that will produce the best benefits. That is the correct application of a tool—to produce the results that you want.

The hardest part for most people is determining just exactly what it is that they do want. They mull around, wish about vacations, complain that they aren't happy, et cetera. Once you know what it is that you are after, you can then select a tool to assist you in gaining your target.

You can benefit from using the Simutrade System if you already trade and want to add greater skill or new strategies without risking your cash until you can become competent. You should see the value of each strategy's Simutrade Worksheet and step-by-step guide at your first glance.

If you are just beginning your portfolio, you can greatly benefit from Simutrading. The Simutrade process is the same whether you have just begun, or you are a seasoned veteran. The beginner, however, may have a few more hurdles to overcome, the main hurdle being having a sufficient amount of capital to start an account. Take heart and be patient. In the meantime, seek out information that will allow you to raise the capital that you desire. Here are some awesome books to help you:

> *The Richest Man in Babylon,* by George S. Clason
>
> *The Wealthy Barber,* by David Chilton
>
> *Think and Grow Rich,* by Napoleon Hill

For the beginner, be warned that Simutrading can be fun. When you make a few good trades and see the value of your Simutrade portfolio increase, it can be exhilarating. You know that if you made the same decisions with real money that you would have cash, instead of a paper increase.

Wherever you are in your trading journey, I welcome you to the Simutrading System.

ACKNOWLEDGMENTS

This book and the concepts in it would not exist, if not for Wade B. Cook, his Speakers, and the people that help them deliver the message, Wade Cook Seminars, Inc.

I'd like to thank all members of Team Wall Street, especially Bob Eldridge, Keven Hart, and all those who have assisted me in producing this book. Thank you, Wade and Laura Cook, for starting me on a new way of thinking and having enough confidence to allow me the opportunity to learn these principles. To my friend, John Childers, thank you for teaching me so many things since my arrival at Wade Cook Seminars.

Special thanks are given to the people at Lighthouse Publishing Group, Inc. who pave the way for new authors.

A special gratitude to David McKinlay, Richard Lowman, and the rest of the Wade Cook Seminars Research/Trading department for their patience, constant enthusiasm, and bold temperament.

Thank you to Brent Magarrell, whose assistance in writing has made this book possible.

To Jay Bird Harris, thank you for helping me everyday to focus on the things of life that are important, both financial and in life, to try to keep me "on track."

THE
BASICS

CHAPTER 1
Tools Of The Trade

For the past 25 years, I have worked in various positions on the railroad and in railroad-related industry. I owned a business that sold goods and services to railroads throughout the country. During those years, our family and business were financially rewarded. In 1988, our sales reached over 10 million dollars. Some time later, I sold the business to a major corporation. I then accepted the position of General Manager of the North Coast Railroad. My position as General Manager required a vast amount of time, energy, and dedication to assist in making the railroad a success. The railroad prospered during my tenure, but our personal family finances were not increasing the way we thought they should. Our financial future really scared my wife and myself as we were at a point where retirement was looming on the horizon.

I have known Wade Cook for some time. About this time, he gave me a copy of his book, *Wall Street Money Machine*. It had already been on the *New York Times Business Best-Seller List* over a year. I read it from cover to cover and thought, "I can do this." It was simple, well presented, and complete. It was exciting to believe that I could even come close to duplicating his results. For the first time, I felt there could be a light at the end of my financial tunnel. I went to a Wall Street Workshop™ seminar and came away with a ton of information. In fact, I had so much information that I didn't know where to start.

Notes:

Notes:

I found that I needed a basic system to practice the strategies without expending all my money—a system with which I could consistently keep track of and review specific trades. The need for a system I could use to learn to make money in the stock market was the beginning of the Simutrade System.

I set up a Simutrade account that allowed me to collect all the information needed. The Simutrade worksheets had blank places to write down the decisions, like why I decided to get into a trade, and when I planned to get out. It could track entire portfolios. Simutrading allowed me to practice the strategies that I learned, but with less stress because I would not lose a penny of my hard earned money. Using Simutrading, I developed my trading skills using actual marketable trades without financial risk. I used my Simutrades to track trades on paper and my real money trades. I had developed a simple tracking system that would allow me to evaluate and examine each trade. I could take apart and examine the details of each trade and see tendencies and patterns in my portfolio.

My evaluation of the trades that I was getting into, however, showed some holes. I was not being consistent. I would have some really good trades, and then some really bad trades. My portfolio was increasing, but not at the rate that I would have liked it to. I knew something was missing from the system.

Then I found the last piece that completes the Simutrade System and makes it glide. It is a good, solid game plan. This is your "gliding guide." It sets a benchmark for you to compare and evaluate each Simutrade. A good game plan can help you to make quick, solid investing decisions. The Simutrade System, with a good game plan, allows you to originate good trades, execute them at a good time, and check your open trades against your game plan criteria. It teaches you the basics of profitable investing.

Please do not underestimate the power of the game plan. It is often the difference between winning and losing. It's the map to your financial destination. Without it, you can easily get lost.

Have you ever heard the phrase "If you fail to plan, you plan to fail?" I believe this to be true. If you do not currently have a plan, then you are most probably failing, or at least not doing as well as you could. Make sure that you devise your game plan. Use the sections in this book that are dedicated to creating a good game plan and fill out the Simutrade Game Plan Worksheet as you go along. This will bring the Simutrading System alive. It is fun to learn to make money, especially when it doesn't take a lot of time.

As you browse the second half of this book you will see a compilation of strategies. Most of these strategies are used in the Wall Street Workshop™ by Wade Cook Seminars, Inc., or taught by Wade and his instructors. If you have not attended a Wall Street Workshop™ or seen one on video, I urge you to do so. The best way to learn any topic is to search out a mentor—someone that has already done what you are setting out to do. Once you find a mentor, learn what he knows and do what he does. This should enable and empower you to achieve the same results.

The Simutrading System is a tool to practice the skills that you need in order to gain the outcome that you want. Although I would like to have included all the possible strategies that are available, I do believe that these strategies (or even one of them) are enough to generate all the cash flow that you desire. If you want an extra $200 a month, you can do that with these strategies. If you want to generate a sizable income, say $25,000 per month, learning the Simutrading System can do that also. If you want to become a millionaire, you can. The Simutrade System is made for you, to be used by you.

Each strategy I explain in *On Track Investing* is a little different than the others and has its own information and evaluation requirements. There is a specific Simutrade Worksheet and Step-By-Step Guide for each strategy. Make sure that you understand the mechanics of a strategy before you start using it. Read the section on each strategy and practice gathering information using the worksheets. Follow the guideline as it is

Notes:

listed. Check them off as you go. Get into the habit of doing this with each trade.

When starting out, I suggest that you use one strategy at a time. You only need to master one strategy to become very wealthy. Using one strategy at a time can also make the evaluation process easier. You can see patterns at a glance and concentrate on solving one problem at a time. If you do use more than one strategy, use a separate tracking system for each one. Once you feel comfortable with the results that you have had on a particular strategy, it may save time and effort to combine your trades into one portfolio. Until then, keep it simple and use one strategy per tracking sheet.

Successful Simutrading gives you the confidence necessary to make good decisions. It increases your understanding of the strategy implementation so that you can profit using cash trades. Make a minimum of 10 Simutrades for each strategy before you use real money in trades. If you have completed 10 Simutrades on a particular strategy and find that you are still not comfortable with the results, I would urge you to check your game plan and seek feedback about the trades you have made. Attend a seminar, read a book, talk to a broker, do something. One of my favorite sayings is, "The true definition of insanity is doing the same thing over and over but expecting different results." If you are not getting the results that you are targeting then you need to change something. Change your entry and exit points. Find better charts. Try more Simutrades.

Always seek information to better your personal trading. You can always improve. The stock market is not a static thing that will be exactly the same year to year. Things change. Make sure you keep on top of things by practicing using new information and techniques with the Simutrade System. Then, evaluate each trade using a benchmark (like your game plan). Adjust your game plan for any problems that you find. Keep doing this process until you are on track.

When you feel confident and on track using Simutrades then it's time to convert to real trades. You will find that the

Simutrade Worksheets will become second nature and your trades will benefit from the use of them.

The Simutrade System is designed to be a depository to collect information quickly, make a decision, and then evaluate the trade to know when to get out. When the trade is done, you also have a device for evaluating results and fine tuning your specific strategy. When applying the Simutrade format, you can use the Stock Transaction Tracking Record for each trade that you want to track. You will find a copy of the Stock Transaction Tracking Record in Appendix 1 of this book. As your understanding becomes more proficient in one strategy, expand your trading arena to include other strategies. To accompany your use of the tracking system, continually review training videos and books, attend seminars, or find other sources of good information to help you understand each strategy more fully. Try to become good, really good, in at least one strategy.

Here is a challenge. Do five or more trades each day. Start out with Simutrades, and then transfer to real trades. You may find that when you use real trades you run out of money before you get to five trades per day. Do as much as you can with real trades and continue using Simutrades with the rest. I am certain that if you do five or more trades per day, for 30 days, your understanding and competence for making money in the stock market will accumulate quickly. In a very short period of time you will be able to originate good trades and create excellent cash flow.

CHAPTER 2
The Game Plan

The most crucial element to a successful, profitable stock market trading campaign is to know what you are doing before you do it. Then do it consistently.

You must know when to get in, when to get out, and why. You need to have a consistent course of action that works.

What a great value it would be if you could have someone available that could make good decisions for you. Simutrading is about making *you* that person.

If you had a map in front of you with your entrance and exit shown in detail and all you had to do is follow the map, could you succeed? If you have a good financial map and you have the skill to follow it, you will get where you want to go financially. The problem then becomes, where do we get our hands on a map to our financial success? For that, we need to tailor our own financial game plan.

Your game plan is like a map of your journey to financial independence through the stock market. If I were to take a trip across the country to a place that I had never been, I would purchase a map. The map would show me which roads to take and guide me to where I want to go. This concept is so simple, yet so crucial. We use maps and plans every day. Have you ever

Notes:

Notes:

gone to a restaurant and ordered from a menu? The menu is a map of the restaurant. It lists what choices are available to you, describes the benefits of each item, and lists the price so that you know what you will be charged before you order. Have you ever gone into a restaurant and said, "Oh, just give me something to eat and charge me whatever you want?" I doubt it.

As investors, we need a map to guide us. Because we can't afford to fail or financially get off track we need a map so detailed that we can know at a moment's glance what we should do, in any situation. I call this investment map a game plan. Before you finish this chapter, you should have a game plan. You can then follow your game plan just like you would a road map until you reach your financial destination.

Once you have a game plan, you need to develop the skills to follow your game plan. This is important. Sometimes we let our emotions get in the way and we make a decision that deviates from our plan. We "hope" that our stock goes up. Do you think that hoping will increase the likelihood of the price of a stock increasing? I doubt it. A successful investor once told me, "Hope rhymes with dope." Maybe this was not very nice, but it is quite true in cases of finance. I believe strongly in intuition and hunches. I believe that there is a part of us that is aware of many, many things that we do not consciously think about. I suggest that you try to listen to these hunches, but make sure that they are in line with your game plan.

I will venture to say that the majority of investors do not have a detailed enough game plan, if they have one at all. They may target a particular strategy with a vague goal in mind, but will end up deciding when to get out after they are already in the trade. The lucky ones eventually learn to use a game plan, have enough money to lose during their learning curve, or just get out of the stock market altogether. For the rest of us who want to succeed and can't afford to fail, we need a game plan.

If you could only learn one thing from this book, it should be to have a plan and practice it. Decide what it is you are doing in the market (or want to do), and *exactly* how you are going to do this. Write it down in the form of a plan—a step-by-step map. Then simply follow your map. If you don't get the results that you want, incrementally modify your plan until you do achieve the desired results.

Sounds simple, doesn't it? Well, I have some good news and some bad news. The good news is that with the correct plan, it is as simple as it sounds. All your decisions can be based upon the criteria you have set in advance. Your map will lead you to your destination. The bad news is that most of the hard work, in the form of financial decisions, needs to be made before you can create your plan. You must decide where you want to go and how you are going to get there.

Let's begin the process of creating a map. Take a look at the Simutrade Game Plan Worksheet on the next page. Fill in the answers that you know right now. Maybe grab another piece of paper and write down the answers as you continue reading this chapter.

The quality of your outcome has a direct correlation to your actions. Like Nike says, "Just Do It!"

We first need a destination. The most common financial destination that I hear is, "I want to be financially independent," or "I want enough money so that I don't have to work ever again." This is not a destination; it is a vague hope. I can't find financial independence on a map because it is not specific enough. We need to have a target to shoot for and then keep that target in our sights.

How specific do you need to be? I can't recall where I read this, but it has stuck out in my mind and surfaces all the time. You need to know what it is that you want, in such detail that if someone were to come across your path and say to you, "I want to make your financial dreams come true. How much, specifically, would you like me to write the check out for?" you would be able to tell that person the exact figure. The more specific that you are, the easier that it can be to concentrate on your trades and not on what you want from your trades.

Notes:

Notes:

SIMUTRADE GAME PLAN WORKSHEET

Starting Point: _____ Date: _____

Destination/Goal: _____
_____

Portfolio Allotment: _____
_____

Trade Allotment: _____
_____

Time Temperament: _____
_____

Strategy(ies): _____
_____
_____

Entry Requirements

Chart: _____ Volume: _____Trend:_____

P/E: _____ Check News: _____

Exit Requirements

Moving Averages: _____ Target Loss: _____

Target Profit: _____

Sources for candidates: _____
_____
_____
_____

Notes: _____
_____
_____
_____

Have you ever heard the expression: "Keep your eye on the ball?" Most people will conjure up an image of a sport that utilizes a ball as the vehicle on which the focus of attention is placed. Baseball is such a sport. A hitter must keep his eye focused on the ball from the moment it leaves the pitcher's hand in order to successfully have the bat strike the ball at the exact moment that it arrives in the strike zone. If the batter is successful, a hit is made. If the batter does not keep his eye in contact with the ball, or if he closes his eyes and hopes, he will probably strike out.

Notes:

I would like you to think of another image. Imagine yourself flying a Navy jet. You are a pilot of one of the fastest vehicles on the face of the planet. You have just successfully flown a mission and are going back to base to get a much-needed rest. You look out your window and see the aircraft carrier floating like a cork out in the middle of the ocean. You as the pilot must land your craft on the deck of the ship. This is your base. In order to land successfully you must use an instrument called a ball. You must keep your eye on the ball. If you use the ball correctly, you will land safely on the deck. If you don't, well, you may end up swimming or sinking yourself and your airplane in the depths of the ocean.

In order to land successfully on that deck, the ball becomes the ultimate instrument to insure that pilot's success. So it is with the stock market. Pick your destination and focus on "keeping your eye on the ball." Your game plan is the ball you must focus on to be successful.

LOCATING YOUR TARGET

One way to find very specific targets is to set goals. I read the book *Think And Grow Rich* by Napoleon Hill a few years ago and have not found its equal in helping me make decisions about what I specifically want. Mr. Hill also explains quite a few techniques that can assist all of us in obtaining our desires and developing your faith.

Another excellent source is Brian Tracy. He has a tape series from Nightingale Connant. Brian poses some thought provoking questions specifically designed to assist your long-term decision making process. He asks, "What one thing would you do in your life if you knew you could not fail?" I believe setting goals are excellent exercises for not only your financial success, but for your emotional well being, spiritual growth, relationships, and whole life.

For a different view on creating a target, try Wade Cook's book entitled *Don't Set Goals*. When I first looked at the cover of this book, I thought to myself, "Now he's done it." As I have

Notes:

read and reread this book I have found his message to be right on track with my way of thinking. How many of us make New Year's resolutions only to find out in March that a quarter of the year has gone by and we have not even thought about our goals, much less taken action to get closer to their fruition. Wade's message is that most people set goals but never achieve them. Don't be a goal setter, be a goal getter. Concentrate on action and direction. The secret in goal achieving is simply, "Just do it!" Taking action towards achieving your goals is key. I strongly recommend this book as required reading. It could help your actions and therefore change your life.

After completing some exercises in goal setting, I came up with 104 solid, specific goals and could not think of one more thing to add. It was a strange feeling knowing what I wanted and having it there in front of me on paper. I was prepared for that mysterious philanthropist and his checkbook. My focus had now changed from what I wanted to how to make those items on my paper into reality. That is where you need to be. Have something to shoot for. Focus your attention on the process of taking action towards hitting the target.

FUNDING YOUR PORTFOLIO

Now that you have a target to shoot for, you must determine where you are shooting from—you have to know your starting point. You could determine your net worth, evaluate your strengths and weaknesses, allot segments of time, et cetera, and then make an educated guess. For now, let's just skip to the educated guess. In Simutrading, what you do with what you have is more important than what you start with. My opinion is to pick an amount that is close to what you have in real money. If you already have a substantial portfolio, then use an amount on the higher end of the scale. I don't know of anyplace where you can open a brokerage account with less than $1,000, so I would not suggest using less. Most investors can simutrade nicely with $5,000 to $25,000.

The purpose of the Simutrading System is to develop the skill of making good investment decisions. Therefore, the amount of your original portfolio should be small enough to still have a target to shoot for, and large enough to make an adequate number of trades.

Can you add or subtract money after you start? Since you will be free to do this when you start using real cash in trades, why not do it the in the Simutrade System? The Simutrade System done successfully will make you wish you had already invested real money!

CHOOSE YOUR VEHICLE

As traders, we use specific strategies to invest our money in order to create more money. The strategy that you use becomes your vehicle with which you travel your map. Choose one strategy and become good at it. Choose one, become an expert vehicle operator, and watch your destination rush into sight and arrive before you know it.

By now, you probably already have a strategy in mind that you want to use. Most people who paper trade have an idea of what they want to do, but need to gain skills and confidence.

I personally like options on Stock Splits. They fit my trading style. They are a short to medium time frame, they have a high profit potential, the downside is capped, and the averages are in my favor as they correlate to the stock price going up.

I also like Rolling Stocks for its simplicity and profit potential. Depending on my criteria for entry into a trade, the risk can potentially be lowered. It also fits within my time requirements.

You need to choose a strategy that fits you. Use that strategy to create your game plan. Then practice using your vehicle until you acquire the confidence to be successful.

WHAT KIND OF TRADER ARE YOU?

One of the decisions that I had to make early on was how much time I had and what effort I needed to expend to accomplish my goals. Some strategies require constant attention,

Notes:

while others just require a casual glance every now and then. For example, Rolling Stocks and Covered Calls are two strategies that fall into the category of less time and less effort compared with other strategies. For Covered Calls, you simply find a stock that meets your purchase criteria. You buy that stock, sell the call and wait until the expiration date. This strategy requires a minimum amount of daily review.

For Rolling Stocks, you find a stock that follows a pre-determined rolling pattern, you purchase the stock at its low point, put in a Good Till Canceled (GTC) order, and wait for the stock to reach its expected sell point (resistance) and your GTC order to be filled. You can then use another GTC order that will allow you to purchase the stock again when it reaches it pre-determined low point (support).

Our time frames will decide which strategy we will follow. Remember: Make the plan, then work the plan. One of the best benefits of using the Simutrade System is being able to judge my "Time Temperament." Time Temperament is your personal character temperament in harmony with a trading time frame and the correct strategy. Let me explain.

A person with short Time Temperament would like day trading. I can imagine them sitting in front of a computer gazing at the screen watching up-to-the-minute quotes on their open trades. They love the anticipation and exhilaration. A short Time Temperament trader may use Stock Split announcements and will most probably will trade Options on News.

A person with a long-term Time Temperament would probably like Rolling Stocks. They would make a solid investment decision requiring only periodic check ups. They might use GTC orders on their exit and maybe even on their entrance. LEAPS® (Long-Term Equity Anticipation Securities) could be in line with a long-term Time Temperament. They can be highly profitable and can take up to two years to play out.

Notes:

I believe there are at least two medium Time Temperaments, maybe even more. One of the best indicators of your Temperament is to use moving averages and determine which work best for you. Following the lead of one of my instructors, I started out using 18 and 21 day moving averages. What I discovered by using them was each time the moving average lines crossed, I would start feeling behind. I was losing too much money in my Simutrades or not getting in soon enough. I wanted to cut my losses to around 20% *maximum*. At the time, I was currently losing up to 40% on some trades. So, after playing around with charts that I was familiar with (I had made some Simutrades and checked up on them most every day), I created different sets of moving averages to see which ones crossed when I would have wanted to get out of the trade. I now use nine and 18 day moving averages, and some five and nine day moving averages. My personal trading style is best suited by these averages. Your Time Temperaments may vary with each strategy you use. Maybe you use five and nine day moving averages when you trade options, and 18 and 21 day moving average when purchasing stock. Find moving averages that are in harmony with your Time Temperament. This, coupled with the correct strategy(ies) will put you into a comfortable, profitable trading pattern.

Please do not underestimate the power of Time Temperament for alleviating a variety of problems. It can be the difference between being happy and content, or increasing the stress in your life, and possibly decreasing the probability of profitable trades because of a bad attitude. You may just have an incorrect trading style that is not in harmony with your personal Time Temperament.

RETURN ON INVESTMENT

Now that we have determined what target we are traveling towards, what strategy vehicle will take us there, and have the Time Temperament that will lend harmony to our trading style, the next step is to target our returns on investments.

How much should you make on each trade? The first time I heard this question, I had difficulty swallowing. I said to myself, "I want to make as much as I can on each and every trade." Well, how do you know when "as much as I can" comes? You don't. You can and should follow the indicators that you select for your strategy and as well as the chart. But, if you target your profit right from the start, you'll know exactly when you get there. This also allows you to use GTC orders. It's really hard to use a GTC if you can't decide what price to put on it. To develop the skill of deciding how to get out before you get in, always target your profit and use a GTC.

I've heard people target 100% on their options plays. I've heard a minimum of 10% on Covered Calls (not including capital gains or being exercised out of your position). I've heard 15% minimum for each roll of a Rolling Stock. You need to decide what is right for you. How conservative are you? Do you have a high tolerance for pain and anxiety? Can you handle more risk?

Whatever you decide, the Simutrade System is focused on making many small, successful trades. Just take out bite sized chunks of profit to add to your cash flow. I feel successful if I make more than 20%. On some trades I want my return on investment to go as high as 100%. My average holding time is between two days and four weeks. Could you live with 20% per month? Even 10% per month is a fantastic return. Using the strategies presented here, 10% is achievable. Some strategies will average more than 10%, some more than 20%, and some even more.

Pick a number that you are comfortable with. Use that as your guide. Build it into your game plan. Don't get greedy. Greediness makes you try to take too big of a bite at a time, you will not be as profitable and potential gains will slip away. I've learned from experience. I had one stock split trade that was up to 129% return on investment (ROI). I asked myself whether I should sell it or not, and I thought, "Maybe I can get 150% or maybe even 200%." Was I getting greedy? Yes. I would have been happy with 20%. I had 129%.

The value of my option decreased sharply and I got out of the trade with a little over 80%. Was I still happy? You bet. I almost doubled my money! However, when I saw the value of my trade go over 100%, which was my upper limit, that was my cue to sell. Don't get greedy. You don't need 100% to become wealthy. Twenty percent can make you very wealthy, very quickly, especially if you compound, or use all your profits to invest in more plays.

MAKE YOUR FAVORITE PORTFOLIO COLOR BE BLUE

The scope of *On Track Investing* is mostly how to keep your money growing for you. Every strategy detailed in this book carries a high risk. Can they create great cash flow? You bet! But we don't want to keep all of our assets in anything that is considered high risk. We need to build up our asset base by purchasing blue chip stocks. These are stocks of some of the greatest companies of our time, and some with the greatest value. Now, I make my home in the Pacific Northwest, so I'll start with some of my home grown favorite blue chips. Microsoft, Boeing, Intel, McDonalds, and Hewlett Packard are all blue chip stocks. Blue chips are those "household name" companies. Everyone knows who you're talking about when you say, "Microsoft," at least anyone who has ever touched a computer. Ever flown in an airplane? Boeing. Ever eaten a Big Mac? McDonalds. *Sleeping Like A Baby*, by John Hudelson, is a great blue chip guide.

I'm a strong advocate of investing in blue chip stocks. After I create a blue chip asset base my next question is: How much should I put into risky strategies? How much should I put into blue chip stocks, and how much into other things?

If you find a good broker, talk over allocation with him. He should be able to give you good advice as to what his brokerage house is recommending as their current portfolio allocation. For the Simutrading System, we assume a new account starting with 100% use for high risk trading. If you start your portfolio balance between $2,000 and $10,000, your gradual shift into blue chips should go something like this:

Notes:

← Book

Portfolio Size	Risk Strategies	Blue Chip
0-$12,000	100%	0
$12,000-30,000	$12,000	Put the rest here.
$30,000-	$15,000-20,000	Put the rest here.

My Simutrade account has increased enough in size that I need to start directing my profits toward the blue chip stocks. See, you can use the Simutrade System to help you determine your portfolio allocation. Start out an account with $30,000 or more. Practice purchasing blue chip stocks. The funny thing about learning to make good buying decisions for the stock market strategies I teach is that in purchasing blue chip stocks, you must look for good entry points.

You may just want to concentrate your attention on the remaining high-risk portion of your account. I say, keep tabs on the blue chips. Look at a chart and check the fundamentals every once in a while. Make sure you know where your money is. Check them as often or as infrequently as you like, but make sure that you do check them.

CREATE YOUR GAME PLAN

By now your game plan should have some blank spaces filled in. You should have your starting point, destination and vehicle, as well as portfolio allotment, target profit and loss (ROI). Let's create an example and fill in one of the worksheets.

This is just an example, and one that we will use later in the chapter on Rolling Stocks and Stock Splits. You need to customize your game plan to suit your needs and trading style. Then start Simutrading. You will soon see whether or not your game plan is on track by the outcome of your trades. Remember that you may need to adjust your game plan so that you can get the results that you want. You may need to sharpen your skills with more knowledge and training. Whatever the situation, use your game plan as your road map. It can take you where you want to go.

SIMUTRADE GAME PLAN WORKSHEET

Starting Point: _____ $5,000 _____   Date: _____

Destination/Goal: _____ $100,000 _____

Portfolio Allotment: _____ 80% safe blue chip investments _____
_____ 20% for all options plays _____

Trade Allotment: _____ Divide by 5, minimum of $1,000 per trade _____

Time Temperament: _____ Medium: 9 and 18 day moving averages _____

Strategy(ies): _____ Call options on Stock Splits, call options on news, _____
Covered Calls, and Rolling Stocks. _____

Entry Requirements

Chart: _ ++++ or better _____   Volume: _ >50,000 _   Trend: _ Upward _

P/E: _ 20 to 80 _____   Check News: _ No bad news _

Exit Requirements

Moving Averages: _ Cross downward _   Target Loss: _ 20% _____

Target Profit: _____ 20 to 100% _____

Sources for candidates: _ Wealth Information Network™ (W.I.N.™), IQ Pager™, _
www.cbsnews.com, yahoo.com split calendar, and Standard & poor split
calendar

Notes: _ Concentrate on getting out early and not getting greedy. _

news

As you look over the Simutrade Game Plan Worksheet, there are still a few things we have not covered—mainly the entry requirements and strategy you will use. Before we dive into the indicators, let's have a look at the single most powerful tool for evaluating your entry, exit and the trade in general. Without this, I would probably not get off the ground as an investment pilot.

I liken our Simutrade System to that of learning to fly a commercial airplane. Before he gets into the cockpit of an airplane, each pilot has had many hours of Simulator Training. Each pilot

Notes:

has many hours of basic instruction, and uses simulator time to practice the basic skills on an unfamiliar aircraft. Would you want a pilot to just jump into a Boeing 777 airplane without training and take off?

The Simutrade System is the opportunity to practice basic skills, become familiar with strategy concepts, and it allows you to get used to making the decisions necessary to make good, consistent, profitable trades. Use Simutrading to become a good investor pilot.

Do you want to risk all of your money? I don't. I want to build up my assets—my net worth—and then manage their growth and protect them from loss. It is one thing to create cash flow and a sizable portfolio. It is an entirely different matter to hold onto that money, protect that money from loss, and then utilize that money to make your desires and dreams come to reality. I hope that you plan for this. Protecting your money is the only way to keep what you make.

 If you want information on asset protection, call Entity Planners, Inc. at 1-800-706-4741. If you don't do anything else, find out about entities and how you can structure them to protect your money, brighten your tax situation, and avoid death taxes. The Nevada Corporation is a must. If you have children, you may want to get a Family Limited Partnership.

CHAPTER 3
Charting Basics

There are many tools available to help you decide whether or not to act on a trade. You want to have a high degree of probable success on the trades that you do act upon. There is one tool that can get the information that you need in front of you for evaluation so quickly that it will make your head spin— a good charting service.

You should not ever spend your money without viewing a chart. Charts show you where a stock's been, the patterns it has, and where it's headed. How are you going to view a chart without a charting service? I guess you could draw your own charts with a pencil, but I don't have the time, patience, nor life span to do that.

The examples described in this book are from TeleChart 2000© by Worden Brothers. I use TeleChart 2000© as a reference to help you understand the basic concepts of charting. TeleChart 2000© has a huge amount of information available right at your fingertips. I like it because of its simple format that doesn't require a doctorate degree to understand.

There are many other sources available. You need to do your own research into charting services to find one that suits your particular needs. Make sure whatever charting service you choose is simple enough to understand that you needn't memorize the whole manual to work it. A quick tour playing around

Notes:

with the software and the menus should lead you to the information that you are looking for.

You will greatly benefit from the study of the instructions given with the charting service software. I encourage you to dive into those concepts thoroughly and use charting to guide you through your game plan with the Simutrade System. Charts can be like a compass, telling you which direction to go. Use them to guide your path.

No matter what charting service you do use, the more familiar you become with this tool, the easier it is to make profitable decisions about the market. You need to get a charting service. Buy one or find one on the Internet. I encourage you, again, to learn its uses. Find out what it can and can't do. You can use all of the feedback that a charting service can provide to make wise decisions. Take enough time to do sufficient research. If you're an old pro at charts, see if my rating system can help you speed through charts faster. Charts help make profitable decisions. Your mastery skill level of the strategies will increase dramatically the more Simutrades you make and the more charts you examine.

THE STRATEGY FOOTPRINT

With a charting service, you can create a picture to correlate with a specific time frame. Pictures can be important, informative, and can show you trends right away. Every strategy in *On Track Investing* has a trend that the individual stocks need to mimic to be good candidates. For example, the Rolling Stocks strategy is used on stocks whose trend is to bounce up and down between two price ranges. If you are looking for good Rolling Stocks candidates, you will look for charts that show this type of trend.

Good news tends to send the price of the stock up by little jumps called "gaps." A good uptrend is like walking up a steep hill. The chart will slowly and predictably move up a little more every day or week, and the moving averages should be going up too.

Look for the specific print that you need for your strategy, then quickly check the rest of the chart to see if your other game plan requirements are met.

Learn the trends that belong to the specific strategies. If you pick them up while the trail is still fresh, you may be able to bring home the game.

Once you learn to detect and track the footprints in the charts, just go hunting. Grab your weapon (Simutrade), put on the high-power scope (charts), and hunt until you find some game. Keep on track by keeping tabs on your chart. This scenario may be a little bit removed from our trading mentality, but the concept is the same.

You can customize how you view charts by specifying guidelines for the charts. Usually, certain indicators are better used with certain strategies. Once you've Simutraded a strategy several times, study some charts of trades you would have liked to have been in and see which indicators were the strongest influences to let you know when to get in.

The greatest value of charts is that they can be viewed rapidly and they provide accurate feedback of information that you need to make decisions. You get to choose the indicators you see, and you can adjust some to your Time Temperament. Then, grab some charts and start reviewing. If you look for trends, you can view many charts within a relatively short time.

With a good charting service you can check all of your open positions in a matter of just a few seconds to minutes. Speed and usefulness of information are two great reasons for using charts. Let's go over some trends, or footprints, and then I'll introduce one of the best chart rating systems available for quick analysis.

Notes:

Notes:

FOOTPRINTS

There is no clear single element that will give you a successful buy/sell signal for any strategy that I'm aware of. It takes a few elements to add up to a good chart, even if there is a footprint. It is, however, quicker to look for the footprint first, then check the rest of the chart and rate it.

The footprint has two categories, the heel and the toe. The toe is the pattern that corresponds to a particular strategy and the heel is the basic foundation that needs to exist for any good trade. Here are some toes:

Resistance: The upper level of a stock's trading range at which a stock's price appears to be limited in upward movement. Resistance is used on Rolling Stocks and other strategies to determine trend.

Support: The lower level of a stock's trading range at which there appears to be a limit on further price declines. Generally, this level is the lowest price that this stock has been trading at. Support is used on Rolling Stocks and other strategies to determine trends.

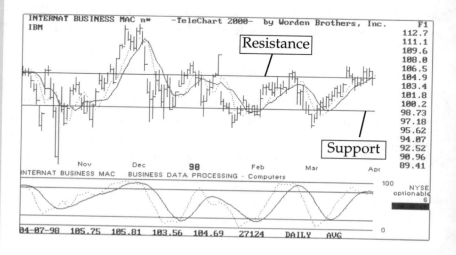

Breakout: This term is shown on the graph when the stock price goes above the resistance level. It breaks upward out of its current pattern or trend.

Breakdown: This term is shown on the graph when the stock price goes below the support level. It breaks downward out of its current pattern or trend.

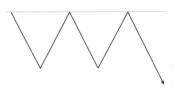

Gaps: Gaps show on charts when the stock's price opens higher or lower than the previous day. This creates a physical gap or space in between opening and closing prices.

In order to use charts effectively with the smallest amount of time and the greatest amount of information, I use a simple rating method of chart evaluation. It is a process to effectively evaluate a chart. The system uses a scoring process with six parameters, they are:

1. Price Graph

2. Stochastics

3. MoneyStream™

4. Balance of Power™

5. Moving Averages

6. Trend

If these factors look good, I score them with a plus (+). If they look poor, I score them with a minus (-). The total number of pluses and minuses on a chart gives the base score. I also like to look at other indicators to make sure other factors are in line. These are "given" and common sense once you figure them out, but must still be checked.

Notes:

Notes:

To show you first hand the power of footprints, here is a "perfect" chart.

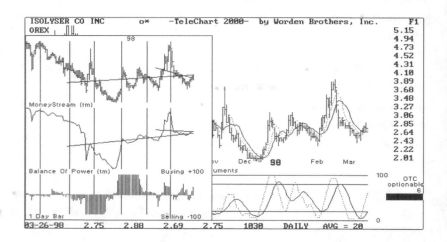

Price Graph: showing stock on weakness = +

Stochastics: crossing at bottom and heading up = +

MoneyStream™: turned up = +

Balance of Power™: accumulation starting = +

Moving Averages: in an uptrend, short, dotted moving average above longer, solid moving average and heading up = +

Volume: over 50,000 = +

Given this picture, do you think that you could find more that are similar? If you can, then you can also find trades that have a high probability of being profitable. Now that we have a visual example to look for, let's go through the chart piece by piece and explain in greater detail what it is that we are actually looking at.

PRICE GRAPH

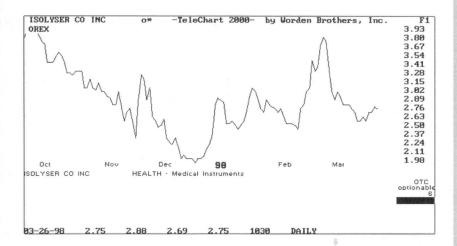

The price graph is a graphical representation of the historical price of the chart. We are simply playing a game of connect the dots. Each dot is the closing price for this particular stock for a specific time frame, usually a day. When all the dots are connected, it creates a picture of the movement of the price of the stock. The connected dots can indicate trends. We can see at a glance if the trend is up, down, or sideways. This is not rocket science, folks, but solid analysis.

We have some choices in terms of the type of price graph we can view. The example above is a simple line graph. This is just a simple connection of the dots. A more sophisticated graph is the bar chart. The bar graph gives more information. Each dot now becomes a small vertical line with a small horizontal line.

The bottom of the line indicates the low of the day. The top of the line indicates the high of day. The small horizontal tick to the right is the closing price of the day. Some charts will also show the opening price with a horizontal tick on the left.

Notes:

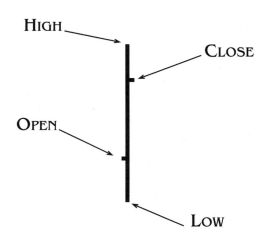

TIME FRAME

The most common time frame is a daily chart. Each dot or bar on the chart equals one day. With one day for each bar we can see a few months on one chart. If you are really interested in a strong trend to support your probability of success, then confirm the trade in another time frame. We can adjust the time frame to two day, three day, one week, one month, et cetera. Viewing a longer time frame can often show us a completely different picture and greatly influence our entry into a trade.

OPEN, HIGH, LOW, AND CLOSE

On the bottom of the screen in TeleChart 2000©, the first number to the right is the price at which the stock opened that morning. The next number is the high for the day. The third number is the low, and the fourth is the closing stock price.

VOLUME

The number next to the closing price is the volume. This number is shown in 100s. You need to add two zeros to find the actual volume. In general practice, you should have a volume of greater than 50,000 before you enter a trade. Make sure to check the average volume by going back for a few days or weeks to confirm the average volume.

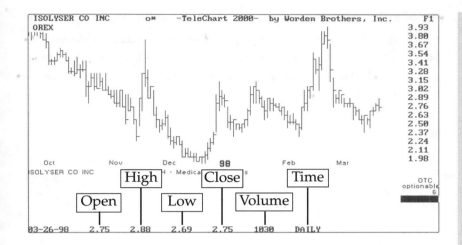

THE HEEL PRINT

When you are looking for strategy footprints, you need to determine what the price of the stock will have to do in order for you to succeed. The basic choice is up or down. If you purchase stock, you want the price of the stock to go up. Similarly, if you buy a call you will benefit most by the price action if the stock takes a strong upward trend. You will be searching for a "positive" chart—one that shows a heel print of an upward price movement.

Opposite the positive chart is the negative chart. The chart is only negative when it doesn't match your strategy. If you were to purchase a put, you would expect to make a profit when the price of the stock goes down. For this scenario, the chart heel pattern is somewhat opposite for the four main rating items. Volume is a constant, so that doesn't change. You still want a good trend, but the trend should be going down if you own puts.

STOCHASTICS

This is a technical indicator showing where the price of a stock is trading within a given range or average. Stochastic lines are found in between the horizontal lines at the bottom third of the chart. For positive rating, the lines must cross at the bottom of the graph in the stochastics area. The green, dotted line will be moving in a vertical direction and will have crossed the red, solid line. If these lines are in the top range or have not crossed, score it as a minus.

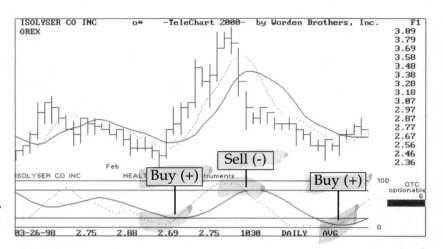

[Note: In the examples in this book, stochastics have been set up with a Period of 14, Moving Average of 7, using green dots, and a Moving Average of 9, an indicator of 2, using solid red.]

MONEYSTREAM™

MoneyStream™ (also Cumulative MoneyStream™ or CMS) is a technical tool developed by Worden Brothers as a cumulative price/volume indicator. Upward sloping lines show patterns in buying and selling of stock. There is a detailed description of MoneyStream™ in the TeleChart© manual.

BALANCE OF POWER™

The Balance of Power™ represents the balance of investors buying stock to those selling stock. The trends are shown by three colors, which are green for positive (high above the buy line), yellow for neutral (right around the buy line), and red for negative (below the buy line). A positive indicator shows that the general trend for the stock activity is buying more then selling. When the Balance of Power™ shows negative, it means that

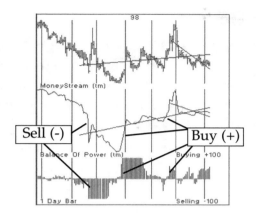

more people are selling right now than are buying. This is sometimes referred to as bleeding because most people are selling the
stock and trying to get out of it. When the Balance of Power™
shows neutral (yellow), this represents that people are being
cautious with the stock. The stock has not moved to positive or
negative. Neutral also does not only mean starting to fall but
can also represent that the stock is on its way back up. Yellow
represents a pivotal movement in the stock, either positive or
negative. Yellow can also signify lack of interest or lack of
volatility in the stock at this time.

How To Score A Chart

Look at each parameter individually and rate it as a plus (+)
for a positive indicator, a zero (0) for a neutral indicator, and
score a minus (-) for a negative indicator.

Each indicator can be viewed for a specific pattern that will
rate as a positive. You need to determine how you will rate each
indicator based on what strategy you are using. If you are buying calls, you want the stock to increase in price. If you are buying puts, you want the stock to decrease in price. The following
scoring instructions are based upon the stock going up. Just
reverse the rating (plus to minus and minus to plus) if your
strategy depends on the stock going down for success. Or, simply go looking for downtrending charts when your strategy
requests.

Notes:

1. PRICE GRAPH

Score this parameter with a plus (+) if the graph shows that the price level is at or near the support level. This means the stock may have bottomed out. Score it a zero (0) if the price is in the mid-range of the graph. Score it a negative (-) if the price is at or above the resistance level.

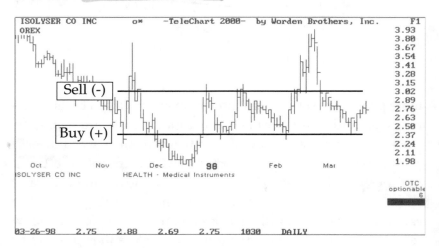

2. STOCHASTICS

If the red solid and green dotted lines have crossed, the green dotted line is pointed up, and one or both lines are in the lower 20% of the lower indicator bar, then score this as a plus (+). If the two lines are moving in the same direction, sideways without crossing, score this as a zero (0). If the green dotted line

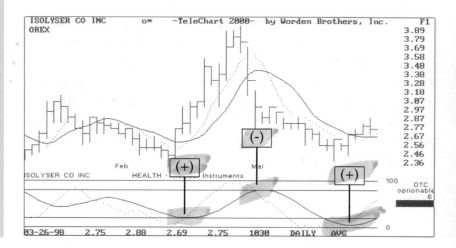

has crossed the red solid line and is headed down, and one or both lines are in the upper 80% of the lower indicator bar, score this as a negative (-).

3. MONEYSTREAM™

The MoneyStream™ lines on the chart indicate the general movement of the stock price. The yellow line shows the new money that is coming into the stock, or that more people are buying the stock. Score this a plus (+) when the yellow line has turned up. Score MoneyStream™ a zero (0) if the yellow line follows the direction of the black line. Score it with a negative mark (-) if the yellow line points downward.

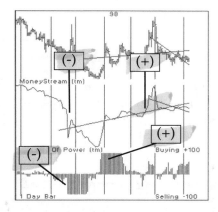

4. BALANCE OF POWER™

Score this parameter a plus (+) if the accumulation indicator is above the black line and green. Score it a zero (0) if the accumulation indicator is yellow. Score it a negative (-) if the accumulation indicator is red.

5. MOVING AVERAGES AND TRENDLINES

You also need to check the current trend. I like to use Moving Averages along with a trend line to indicate the current trend. If the trend is up and the price graph shows a breakout (crossing the resistance line), then you can score the trend a plus (+). You can also score the trend a plus if the short moving average (usually green and dotted) is above the longer moving average (usually red and solid) and both are rising. If the trend

Notes:

is flat and not really going anywhere, score a zero (0). If the trend is heading down, the longer moving average is above the shorter moving average, score this as a minus (-).

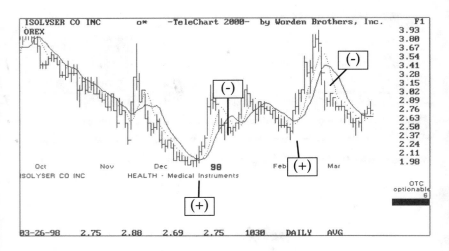

[Note: Most examples in the book have been shown with a short moving average of 5, price indicator 1, with green dots, and a longer moving average of 9, price indicator 1, with a red solid line.]

6. VOLUME

You generally want to see volume over 50,000. If the volume is more than 50,000, this parameter is a plus (+). If the number of shares indicator is right around 50,000, score it a zero (0). If the volume is below 50,000, score it a negative (-).

For my own personal trading style, if I have a negative volume indicator, I usually don't take action on the trade. The stock just doesn't have enough people interested to warrant getting in. You don't want to be the whole market on one particular position. It is also a good rule of thumb to keep the quantity of shares purchased (or options) to less than 10% of the volume. Therefore, if the volume were around 50,000 you would not want to buy more than 5,000 shares.

EVEN MORE CHART INDICATORS

There are many indicators that you can look at other than the ones listed above. Seek them out. Try them to see how they work. Read about them. Discover which ones work for you. One that I've been hearing more and more about is MACD or Moving Average Convergence/Divergence. Here is a brief synopsis by Dr. George Park of the Wade Cook Research and Trading Department:

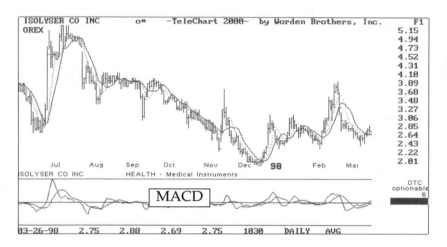

MACD

MACD refers to an oscillator technique that uses two exponentially smoothed moving averages. The Moving Average Convergence/Divergence trading method (MACD) is attributed to Geral Appel of Signalert Corporation (Great Neck, NJ 11021). It is my favorite technical indicator because it gives powerful buy and sell signals which lead and, therefore, predict the price action of a given stock. "Exponentially smooth" means the computer uses a mathematical formula to make the oscillator lines easy to read. These moving averages revolve above and below a zero line. The most useful signals are given when the faster line crosses the lower line, and vice versa. A "buy" signal occurs when the shorter (by time) line crosses above the longer (again by time) line and a sell signal when it crosses below the slower line. Each signal is confirmed on the crossing of the zero line. These moving averages can also be used to help spot turns in the trend. An ideal buy signal would be seen on a bullish divergence, accompanied by an upside crossing by the shorter average and then a crossing above the zero line by both averages. An ideal sell signal would be the reverse of the buy signal.

NOW SCORE THE CHART

On each Simutrade Worksheet you will find a box with the space provided for you to score your chart. Put your plus, minus, and zero marks on the appropriate line. After you are done, look at all the indicators, add them up and write the total (or use + and - symbols) to give the chart an overall score.

With this system you have a possible score range of six positive indicators (++++++) to six negative indicators (------). Generally, you use the first four indicators listed above to determine your base score. Then you can add trend and volume as two additional pluses. What you really want to see is four or more pluses for a base score.

A four (or more) plus chart (++++) means all the base parameters have been rated a plus. A four plus stock is a stock that you should play after checking the news. Be careful though because the chart is only one factor. Check any news, check the rumors, check bulletin board services such as the Wealth Information Network™, and check with your broker. Make sure that you don't use the charting system without some fundamental analysis. If you purchase the new TeleChart 2000© for Windows 4.0, you can include the fundamentals with your charting. Worden Brothers have introduced fundamentals for each stock! All the information that you need is in one simple, easy place.

A three plus chart (+++) is a stock that you will probably play depending upon other indicators that are listed above. You could have three plus base rating and then a plus for volume and a plus for trend. This would be a good playable trade. If you only score three pluses (+++) (volume and trend are zero or negative), then this could still be a playable trade.

A two plus chart (++) should be placed on your frequently checked watch list. This is not the best time to get into this trade. Not enough factors have come into play yet. Give the chart some time to develop. Check it every so often to see if the rating has gone up to a three or a four plus chart.

A one plus chart (+) is a stock that can be watched less frequently. You may or may not want to put this chart in your watch list. It may be better use of your time to watch and search for better charts.

A chart that has a rating of zero (0) should be thrown away. There isn't enough going on. Remember that some strategies use positive indicators and some use negative indicators. None of the strategies employed use a zero as a good buy signal. If you find a zero, move on and find another trade.

Keep in mind when scoring that pluses and negatives cancel each other out and that zeros are neutrals.

Don't buy less than three plus (+++).

Read that above sentence again, memorize it, and adhere to it. If you want to originate good trades, make sure that your technical analysis shows you a good solid "technical" reason to buy. If you can't find any three or more plus charts, move on and wait. It's not worth the risk.

Let's look at some examples. Since the inside of this book is black and white, you may have to look a little harder to evaluate your indicators. In real-life charting, the added dimension of color helps enormously. Generally, I like to set up TeleChart 2000© so that green is go, or buy, and red is stop, or don't buy.

EVALUATE YOUR OPEN TRADES WITH THE SCORING SYSTEM

It would be nice to make a purchase decision and have the trade perform just like you want it to. Some will, some won't. You can use the chart scoring system to keep up-to-date with your open positions. If you have entered a trade on a four plus

Notes:

Notes:

(++++) chart, make sure that you check it periodically for signs of change. I usually try to view the charts of my open positions at least once a day. If my four plus chart goes down to a two plus chart, I need to re-evaluate the trade, maybe go through the Simutrade process, or exit the trade.

This is one of those things that you need to turn into a habit. Don't hope that the stock will turn around. Remember, "hope rhymes with dope." If the stock takes a downward trend, the charting indicators will notify you and you can re-evaluate the trade to see if you want to get out. It might be a good deal again later, but don't base your decision on hope. It would be better to get out now and take a little profit, than to hope the trend will recover and it doesn't. Just get out, and watch the charts. If you get a good buy signal again, get back in. If not, move on to the next trade. Don't risk more than you have to.

Sometimes, I think of days as "surfing" charts. You want to ride the waves up, and coast the downsides. Buy and ride the trend upward and have fun surfing. If your wave dissipates or crashes, change directions and go looking for another wave. Just like the ocean always has waves, the stock market always has potentially good trades. Which trade you choose to do, and with which strategy, produces the result.

WATCH LISTS AND SEARCH ENGINES

If you want to watch a specific wave as it goes up and down, just look at a chart. It looks like a wave cut crosswise. When the wave is at the bottom, start looking for a signal to buy with your strategy that matches.

Most charting programs have a feature that can "watch" a lists of stocks. You can create a category, like Rolling Stocks, that you can place ticker symbols into and track potential future trades. Just pull up your watch list and see all the potential stocks you have and view where the wave is you want to catch.

Maybe the chart is not quite giving you a buy signal, but the current trend indicates that in the near future things could change and the rating of the chart could go up. Put this chart into a "hot" watch list and check the charts more often.

With watch lists you can categorize things to match your style. Maybe you are a good time manager. Set up your watch lists by how often you want to look at certain charts. Have some monthly, some weekly, and some daily. If you're an intra-day trader, you may have hourly watch lists, or certain stocks that you want to view at a specific time, like just before the close of the market. This charting method is fairly simple and, when you use it, can be very, very powerful.

How do you get candidates to put into your lists? I like to call this process the "Search Engine." I mostly equate a search engine with a type of computer software that, given criteria that you specify, can go search for and return the information to you.

TeleChart 2000© has a search engine. You can find Peaks and Slams by entering a range of a price jump, either up, down, or both, and having the software look through all your charts and report back to you which ones that it found. It can even put them into a watch list for you. Then you can view each chart individually and rate the chart. Pick the best few and take the next step, like check out fundamentals. TeleChart 2000© can now search Price/Earnings Ratios. If you want to find good charts with good earnings behind the company, just determine what you want your P/E Ratio to be, say 20, and have the search engine report back to you only the Slams with better than 20.

However, sometimes the best search engine is you. You can look for the information that you want in the format that you want it in. What about Stock Splits? Let's say you choose to employ Stock Splits Strategy Entry Point 4. This play is based upon the date of the actual split. This is usually weeks after the announcement is made public and everyone knows about it. Why not just find a source that tells us the information that we need to know so we can create a watch list with those splits?

Notes:

Here are a couple that have sites on the Web:

www.stockinfo.standardpoor.com

www.yahoo.com

What about news? The best way, in my opinion, to get news fast is through a stock market pager service. It can go with you wherever you go. There are some limitations, however. You only get certain bits of information. Then you need a source of more detailed information. Find a news site on the Web that you like and use it in correlation with your pager.

There are a lot of newsy websites out there. Newspapers like *USA Today,* stock related companies like Standard & Poor, private newsletters, news services, e-mail news services, and even some individual stock market traders, have websites.

CHAPTER 4

Indicators, Factors, And Rules To Live By

This chapter is dedicated to some basic information and some miscellaneous facts. I hope the information here can fill in some holes and clarify some concepts.

PLAY THE STRATEGY, NOT THE STOCK

The word strategy, as I understand it, means a set of rules, or factors, that when followed produce desired results. The strategy is a process. You need to concentrate your attention on the strategy first, then go and find stocks that match the strategy criteria.

Bringing our personal likes and dislikes about a company, is a common error when deciding on a trade. It would be backwards to find a stock and then try to pigeonhole it into a particular strategy. There is also a tendency, especially when you take a loss, to make yourself determined to make money on a particular stock for reasons other than it being a good strategy candidate.

Maybe you think that Microsoft is an awesome company and that you should be able to make money buying Microsoft stock. That may or may not be true, but why not use the strategy first. If Microsoft happens to fit your strategy, by all means, go for it. If it doesn't fit, don't force it.

Notes:

A common mistake is that when you lose money on a particular stock, your tendency is to want to recoup your losses on that particular stock. Why? Revenge has no impact on the stock itself. Options have no joy. Covered Calls do not get depressed. Stock Splits do not have multiple personality disorders. We, as human beings, are the ones with emotions. We need to keep this in perspective.

Also, try not to be led by your emotions when making investment decisions. Don't get me wrong. I highly value emotions and believe that they are an integral part of life. Without our emotions of happiness, sadness, loneliness, and bliss, this world would indeed be a dull place to live.

However, emotions tend to get in the way in investing. You can get really happy about a particular trade. This may sway you from getting out at your pre-arranged exit point. You may believe that the stock is going to go up another 10 or 20 points, but if you have arrived at your exit point, get out. If the trade looks that good, maybe it still is within your game plan. If so, just wait for another buy signal and get in again.

Three rules of strategies:

1. If you don't have a clear buy signal, don't enter the trade.

2. If it is not part of your game plan, don't enter the trade.

3. If you don't know your exit points—your target profit and target loss—don't enter the trade.

Only buy when you know your selling point. If you can determine your selling point, and place a GTC, what is left for you to do? Just check the stock periodically to make sure the trend is still in your favor. Check the moving averages. Check and make sure that your targeted loss has not been reached. If everything goes as planned, your GTC order will be filled. You will have hit your target directly—a bull's-eye.

In order to hit the bull's-eye, you must be able to see it and focus your attention on it. Know by just a simple comparison of two numbers whether to invest or not. Use yes or no questions. If you target your loss at 20%, figure out exactly what that means. If you have a $10 stock, 20% would be $2. If your $10 stock becomes an $8 stock, you need to exit the trade. No ifs, ands, or buts, just exit, sell, buy, or whatever it is to close out your position.

GTCs are like sighting out a target bull's-eye and letting loose an arrow. We may have to wait to see if the arrow hits, but the concept can be the same. The point is to have set targets, to know your outcome, to know when and if you get out before you enter the trade. This is like a trading ninja tool. It seems that only the people that get to be good at these strategies understand and implement this skill.

There is the element of hunch, or intuition. I mostly use this as a gut feeling *not* to get into a trade. If the indicators are showing me the green light, but something tells me not to enter the trade, I don't enter the trade. The reverse, however, is not true. If the indicators are showing me a red light, and there is not a clear buy signal, don't get into the trade no matter what your emotions and intuition tell you. The best trades happen when you have a good buy signal *and* you feel good about the trade.

The way to overcome the emotional factor in investing is to concentrate on the logic of the strategy. Go through the process one step at a time, and then evaluate the trade with the criteria on your game plan. If the strategy process gives you the green light, enter the trade (of course, after you have already determined your exit).

FUNDAMENTAL ANALYSIS

It is a good idea to use Fundamental Analysis in evaluating your potential position. Up to this point, we have been talking about technical analysis—charting and adhering to a strategy. Fundamental analysis can tell us something about the company we are investing in.

Here are some fundamentals and a brief definition:

1. ***Earnings or P/E Ratio***: Earnings show us the state of the cash flow of the company that we are investing in. I've heard it said that cash flow is the lifeblood of a business. Without it, you can bleed to death.

Price tends to follow earnings. If the cash flow decreases, it logically follows that the price of the stock will most likely decrease. The company will not have cash flow to pay for things like investment for growth, excess debt reduction, paying taxes, and a host of other things. Without the cash to pay for things, most businesses have a difficult time operating smoothly, if they can operate at all.

Most of the time earnings are shown in the form of a Price to Earnings Ratio. You figure this by dividing the earnings per share into the price of the stock to get a percentage.

There is no magic number for earnings. There are, however, factors to consider when you look at the P/E Ratio. What sector is the company in? What are the standard P/E ratios for the stock's competition? Are there earnings for the last twelve months, or are they projected earnings? I would say that a good benchmark for earnings is to look at some indexes, like Standard & Poor 500. See what the average P/E Ratio is. Only invest in companies that have a P/E Ratio of 40 or less.

If you want, you can get more "fundamental" and research the earnings of a company more fully (This is also available on W.I.N.™). Look at the P/E for the "sector" or other businesses that do a similar kind of business. Research the average P/E for the stock exchange that your stock trades on. Most brokers have access to P/E Ratios and can tell you what the average ratio is for other companies doing the same kind of business. Have a peek at their financial statements. This alone can reveal oodles of information.

If you follow good earnings, you add more percentage points to the probability that your trade is going to be successful. If you will look on the Simutrade Worksheets, you will notice a place to put the P/E Ratio for the company. You may want to give a good ratio a plus (+), an okay ratio a zero (0), and a high ratio a minus (-). For me, I try and stay away from companies with high ratios. The stock is probably overvalued and I don't want to pay more than something is worth. Earnings are a solid indicator and will not let you down. Avoid investing in companies with a high P/E Ratio.

2. **Return On Equity:** Return on stock equity is a way of calculating the company's after-tax profits divided by the book value. What you want to see is this figure increase year by year.

3. **Debt Ratio:** This fundamental shows how much money the company owes compared to the equity of the shareholders. As you can guess, the less debt a company has, the better off the company is going to be if it runs into hard times. It's just like our personal finances. If your bills are almost the same as your income, what happens if something happens to your income level? Well, you simply can't pay all of your bills. If your debt ratio was low, say for every $100 dollars that you took in you only had to pay out $20 in debt, how would that be different if your cash decreased? It would be much easier to keep current on your bills. So it is with corporations. You want to see low debt ratios. You want to target the debt ratio of companies you invest in to be under 30%. If a company's debt ratio is 50% or high, move on to another deal. It's just not safe.

4. **Cash Dividends:** Companies sometimes pay out dividends in the form of cash to shareholders. There is actually a strategy called Dividend Capturing where you search out companies that pay dividends, purchase the stock just before the dividend is paid, receive the dividend, then sell the stock. You receive a Return On Investment (ROI) that is equal to the dividend. You count the time lapse for this strategy in days. Cash Dividends are not a major factor in the overall scheme of

Notes:

things. However, if a company pays out a good dividend, it would appear to me to be better than a company that does not. Do research on your own if this interests you.

5. **Book Value:** This fundamental answers the question, "What is the company really worth?" This is the dollar amount that you get when you subtract all the liabilities from the assets. You then divide this amount by the number of outstanding shares. This is the "real" value of the shares. You can imagine Book Value as what you would get as a shareholder if the company decided to close its doors and stop doing business, then liquidated its assets and dispersed this sum to the shareholders.

MARGIN

It is possible to have more buying power than you have money available. You can spend more than you have. Buying power is the money that you can use right now to purchase stock, money that is not being used on another trade. In a regular brokerage account, your buying power is the difference between the amount of money you have in your account minus the amount that you have spent on open trades.

Being able to buy on margin is like getting a line of credit at the bank. You can now use somebody else's money and pay them back later with some interest for the service. If you don't already have a margin account, ask your broker about margin requirements—what does it take to open a margin account?

Why would you want to have a margin account and use someone else's money? One simple little answer: higher yield. If you purchase 1,000 shares of stock at $7 per share, that would be $7,000. If you had a margin account you may be able to only put up half the money. Now your cost on the 1,000 shares would be $3,500 ($7,000 divided by half equals $3,500). Or, you could still use $7,000, but now you could buy 2,000 shares. You have just created the potential of doubling your rate of return and your yield.

You must employ good money management principles with a margin account. The broker lending you the money will let you keep the profits of the trade. All he wants is interest. You pay him a going rate, maybe 8% annual interest, and he stays happy with you keeping the profit. However, if you take a loss, that's your responsibility. One of the worst things about a margin account is a Margin Call—you receive a telephone call from your broker telling you that you must deposit more money into your account to cover the trade. If you employ good money management techniques, like always leave 25% buying power, then you can avoid margin calls.

You can't buy options on margin. I would not want to anyway, as they pose more risk. A margin account can double your profits, but can also increase loss on the downside. It's best to use safer strategies to purchase on margin. Try using a Margin Simutrade account utilizing Covered Calls and Rolling Stocks. This way, you can experience first hand the wonders of margin, without experiencing the downside.

Notes:

CHAPTER 5
On Options

In order to understand the basics of the strategies that use options, it is important to understand what stock options are and how they work. For the beginner, options can be very intimidating if you don't understand the jargon. There are certain words that seem to have a whole life in options, but nowhere else. With that in mind, let's briefly dive into some generalities about options.

The first time that I was introduced to the concept of options, I was reminded of an accounting class where I learned about debits and credits. The concept was rather simple, but the terms seemed to be elusive to the normal intellect. I knew how to add or subtract a number to get the correct sum, but do you subtract a credit from an equity account, or add a debit to an expense account? It seemed to be non-intuitive.

If you can grasp hold and memorize a few basic concepts concerning options, it will open the doors to understanding and you can get on to serious Simutrading. If you do not know these terms, I suggest that you do not trade with options until you do. It could make that much difference. Can you make money without understanding options? Yes, you can. In order to have consistent profitable trades with options, however, you need to understand the basics. Learn as much as you can. If you are going to employ option strategies, then learn the basics thor-

Notes:

51

oughly so that they are second nature to you. This can help you to sleep at night without worrying about your out-of-the-money naked put.

If you already know these terms, just keep on reading. Make sure that you not only understand, but also can give an intelligible explanation of all the terms that follow.

Option: An option is a contract that gives to the purchaser the right, *not the obligation*, to buy or sell a stock on or before a certain date at a specific price.

Strike Price: The specific price that you can buy or sell your stock for is called the Strike Price.

Exercised: Because owning a call or a put gives you the right, but not the obligation, to buy or sell a stock, many options are never used. When they are used, it is said that the option has been exercised.

Expiration Date: The third Saturday of the month is the expiration date. All options are written for a specific month (i.e., a December $45 Call). Options are time dependent and will expire with no value on the expiration date (ex-date) for the month that they are written for. Options are like an ice cube—they melt away and disappear—they evaporate. This is one of the major differences between stocks and options.

Increment: The prices available for purchasing options have certain preset increments. If the stock price is between $5 and $25, the options will sell in increments of $2.50. If the stock price is between $25 and $200, the options will sell in increments of $5. Beyond $200, the increments sell for $10.

Call: A call option is the right, *not the obligation*, to buy stock on or before a certain date at a specific strike price. When you purchase a July $45 Call, you are paying for the right to buy the stock at $45 per share by the ex-date in July.

Put: A put option is the right, *not the obligation*, to sell stock on or before a certain date at a specific strike price. When you purchase a July $45 Put, you are paying for the right to sell the stock at $45 per share by the ex-date in July.

Since you can not only buy calls and puts, you can also sell them, this adds up to four basic strategies for options.

Buy a Call: You pay for the right to buy, or "call away," stock from someone else. If exercised, you own stock that you didn't own before, for the strike price of the call. You want an uptrending chart to buy a call.

Buy a Put: You pay for the right to sell the stock to someone, or you "put" the stock to them. If exercised, stock that you own will be owned by the person who bought your put at the strike price. You want a downtrending chart to buy a put.

Sell a Call: You are paid a premium for someone to have the right to buy stock from you. If exercised, you will have the stock bought from you at the strike price.

Sell a Put: You are paid a premium for someone to sell stock to you, for someone to "put" it to you. If exercised, you must purchase stock for the strike price.

Options are like using someone else's stock as collateral, or leveraging your money. You are increasing your buying power. Before options, if you wanted to control 1,000 shares of stock, you would have to go and purchase the stock. Now, with options, you can buy options and thus control 1,000 shares of stock for a fraction of the price. Options are profitable because you can make as much profit from owning the option as you would from owning the stock.

All options are fixed-time investments and thus inherently extremely risky. That is, your options will expire on a certain date. This is called the expiration date. In the United States all options for the particular month expire on the third Saturday of the month. Since the market is closed on Saturdays, all trades will have played out by the close of business on Friday. When an option expires, it is worthless. It has no value and is expired. This is the risk of options. You must do something with your

Notes:

investment, either sell it or exercise it, otherwise it will become worthless and you will have lost the money that you used to pay for the option. Make sure you understand the basics to avoid ending up with an expired, worthless option. Choose your exit and follow your game plan.

Generally, we purchase an option in order to sell it at a profit. We usually don't want to actually own any stock. We want to invest in the option, have the option go up in value, then sell the option for a profit.

When you own an option contract, it gives you the right to buy or sell the stock that the option is written for. This is called a derivative. You don't actually own the stock, but a contract that controls some stock. Options are an expanding market. You can buy options on stock, options on indexes, options on mutual funds, and maybe one day they will get confused enough to create options on options.

There are, however, some good advantages to investing in options. The number one reason is the amount of leverage that you get. If you were to purchase 1,000 shares of a stock that had a price of $100 per share, you would have to fork out $100,000. That's a lot of money for one trade, unless you happen to have a very large portfolio. How about purchasing an option on that same security. If you were to purchase 10 contracts (options are sold in contracts of 100) on the same stock, you might only have to pay something like $5,000. See the difference?

When you get a quote for an option, the price that you get will be something like $1^1/$_2$ or $3^1/$_4$ per share. Contracts are sold in 100 share increments, so if you purchase an option at $3^1/$_4$, you would pay $325 for one contract and control 100 shares. In the example in the previous paragraph, our price was $5 per share. That's $5 per share times 100 (each contract is in an increment of 100 shares) equals $500 per contract. We purchased 10 contracts times $500 per contract, or $5,000.

Can you see the advantage to our pocketbooks when we purchase options? We get more bang for our buck. We can capitalize on the movement of the stock without paying a high price for each share.

Another good thing about options is that you can only lose as much money as you put in. No more. If you purchase an option for $700, then that is the maximum amount that you can lose. Remember portfolio allocation? Because options have a melting factor and you can lose 100% of your investment, we need to control the amount of our overall portfolio that is expended in options.

To offset your potential for loss, options have an unlimited upside potential. The value of your option has no ceiling to limit its increase, except supply and demand. The value of an option can double or triple while the stock goes up just a few dollars. If the stock takes off like a rocket with its price heading up and up and up, guess what happens to the value of the option? It skyrockets too.

What is the difference between purchasing the stock and purchasing the options, and why would someone want to purchase an option and increase their risk when they could just purchase the stock itself?

EXAMPLE 1:

> *Buy 1,000 shares at $100 per share. Cost: $100,000.*
> *Stock goes up to $110 per share*
> *Profit: $10 per share times 1,000 shares equals $10,000*
> *ROI: $10,000 divided by $100,000 equals 10%.*

Not bad. But look what happens if we purchase the options.

EXAMPLE 2:

> *Buy 10 call contracts at $5 for $100 strike price. Cost: $5,000*
> *($5 times 100 (each contract) equals $500 times 10 contracts equals $5,000.)*
> *Stock goes up to $110.*
> *Option goes up to $10 each.*
> *Profit: $5 times 100 (each contract) equals $500 times 10 contracts equals $5,000.*

At first glance, it might appear that we made more money purchasing the stock. Before you decide, let's look at our ROI:

ROI: $5,000 divided by $5,000 equals 100%

We have doubled our money. Now, which would you rather have? Invest $100,000 at 10% and receive $10,000 or invest $5,000 at 100% and receive an additional $5,000?

I don't know about you, but I'd take the 100% any day. Less of my money was at risk, plus I could use that other $95,000 to invest in other things. By purchasing options I have leveraged my money to work harder for me on the same stock. The only difference was that I purchased an option and not the stock.

Please keep in mind that options are risky. For instance, bad news can kill an option. Imagine for a moment that we purchased our 10 contracts for $5,000. Then, the next day some bad news came out about the company. Maybe they just got into a big lawsuit, or maybe the government has come in and halted their business. Whatever the news, let's imagine that it's bad.

The stock falls to $90, then to $80 and goes all the way down to $69. The chance of the price of the stock getting back to $100 is not good, and if it did get to $100, you may not even break even! Your $5,000 in essence has vanished, "Poof." On expiration day, it will expire worthless.

See, the risk factor is high. Options can be volatile. The flip side of the coin is that options also have a potential for large gains. It's very common for options (like Options on Stock Splits) to double and maybe triple in value. You don't often see a stock double in value, and almost never triple in value, especially in a short period of time like two weeks. Options can, and do, double often.

Remember to use portfolio allocation when using options. This is of paramount importance. You need to protect your assets. Don't risk it if it is not prudent. In my opinion, since options have such a high probability to have high increases, I can allot 10% of my portfolio to them. One step further, divvy up that 10% over quite a few trades. If you have $100,000 in your portfolio and are going to dog-ear $10,000 for options (10% of $100,000), I would suggest buying 10 different options for $1,000 each. I might go as high as five positions at $2,000, but no more. This spreads the risk factor out. If one company has bad news, you may lose a good percentage before you stop out. However, there is also a good chance that one of your positions could have really good news and that option can increase and make up for your loser trade.

I really like options. They allow the small investor the chance to invest in stock that they might not have the capital to invest in otherwise. I also like the potential for high profit. I don't mind risking a small percent of my portfolio for a potentially big gain. As a matter of fact, I believe that options are a great source of cash flow.

Make sure that you know what you're getting into before investing in options. Read the pamphlet put out by the Chicago Board of Exchange called *Characteristics and Risks of Standardized Option*s. Talk to your broker. Attend an options seminar. Read a book.

I attended an excellent options seminar called High Octane Options, by Steve Wirrick. Boy, if you want to see a guy who knows options, who lives, eats and breathes options, go see Steve. You'll be glad that you did, and I would venture to bet that your portfolio will be glad, too.

Notes:

CHAPTER 6

Damage Control And Money Management

One of the most important concepts taught concerning the stock market is how to avoid losing money. If you can learn how to lessen your losses, you will be able to keep more of your money in profitable investments. Remember and memorize this quote; it is the basis for controlling your losses:

"Know your exit before you ever go in the entrance"
—Wade B. Cook

This chapter is about cutting your losses. You need to know when to get out of trades that are not performing according to your game plan. This may be one of the hardest skills to acquire and yet one of the most important. If you can master this skill, you can decrease stress and make your whole investing life a safe, sane, and happy time.

Imagine that you have five open positions. Three are going up nicely, taking incremental up ticks, and making you money. Your other two trades are losing. One is slipping just a little. The other has taken a dive. The loss from this one diving trade eats up all the profits in the other trades. Does this happen? You bet it does. It happens all too often.

One of the best ways to cut your losses would be to have a game plan with your targeted losses included. Yes, that's right, I said to target your losses. Why would you target loss? Isn't the name of the game to make a profit?

Notes:

59

Are *all* your trades going to be profitable? Certainly not. Will you make a profit each time that you invest your money? I doubt it. If you never lose, please get in touch with me so that I can learn what you are doing! Now brace yourself—you are going to lose on some trades. It is fact. So, why not plan on it and put it in your game plan.

If you know in advance that you are going to lose on some trades, why not set a target limit to your loss before you lose? When you reach that mark, get out of the trade. Practice this. Get good at it.

The thing I like least about trading is losing money. At one point in time, I started having more successful trades than I did losing trades, but my overall portfolio was only inching up in value. My losses averaged between 15 and 40%. I even had a few that lost 70% or more. Ouch! This bothered me a lot. I modified my game plan to target a loss of 20% or less on any one trade. I practice this hard. To me this is a very important skill. If I can cap my losses at under 20% and I target a 20 to 100% return, which way should my portfolio go? Up, way up.

An excellent source for cutting losses is to use moving averages. We have already covered moving averages in a previous chapter. If you don't understand them yet, go back and read everything on moving averages again. If you still cannot grasp the concept, go get another source of information. Study and use moving averages until they are useful to you. They can be a powerful visual indicator.

When you use two moving averages and your stock is in an uptrend, the shorter of the two moving averages should be on top of the longer moving average. When the shorter moving average crosses through and heads below the longer moving average, get out of the trade. Don't second-guess, don't hope, and don't try to convince yourself into believing that it is not happening. Get out of the trade.

There is one school of thought that says you have one extra day for the closing price to recover above the longer red moving average. Do not let the closing price, under any circumstance, close below the longer moving average for more than two days without getting out of the trade. If you have to take a loss, do it. If you haven't yet reached your target profit, forget it. Take what profit you can and get out of the trade.

There are not many guarantees in investing, but this comes as close as you can get. Again, when the closing price falls below your long moving average, close out your position and move on to the next trade.

If you can follow this one simple rule, you can significantly cut your losses. Just for fun, go look at as many charts as it takes to convince you of this factor. Check what happened to the trend when the closing price crossed the long moving average. Live by it. Profit by it.

EXAMPLE 1

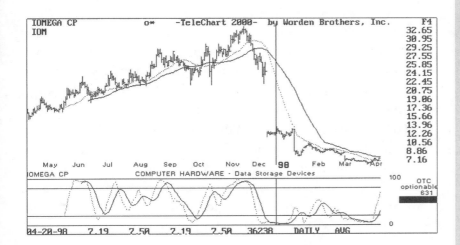

Occasionally we read charts on stocks that look like excellent candidates to purchase, but they do not turn out as we expect. Let me show you a personal example of how I handled a particular situation.

My first trade after attending the Wall Street Workshop™ was on a company called Iomega (ticker: IOM). I purchased 200 shares at $26. I sold the call for a premium of $2.38. This was using the Covered Call strategy that I learned in class.

Notes:

Two days later the stock dropped like a rock to $17. Of course my wife congratulated me on making such a fine trade and it caused quite a stir in my household. The stir continued when Iomega dropped to $15. I don't always recommend the following scenario on every play that has lost money, but the concept can be considered.

When a stock starts to lose money, a stop loss order can be placed. This can be done especially if you know your exit at your entrance. If you think the stock has a chance to recover at some time, consider the following.

Iomega at the time was very volatile and had swings above and below my strike price of $30. I watched the stock go from $26 to finally bottoming out at about $13.50. On the way down I purchased 600 more shares. Two hundred more were purchased at $17.50 and calls at that same strike price were sold for a premium of about $1.50. It continued down so that at $15, I purchased 200 more shares and sold another call at $1.25. It went to $13.50 and I bought 200 more shares and sold more calls at $1. All the options I purchased were to expire in the next month, about 40 days later. Almost immediately after purchasing the last stock for $13.50, the stock started to climb back up. When expiration day finally arrived, my initial loss was negated and actually I had made about $300. The stock had climbed back to $21. I felt the stock had a good potential and chose to ride it out. My hunch was correct. On some stocks you may chose to get out and not ride out the wave. A great plan is to look at the news of the company to enhance your ability to analyze your course of action. Then work your plan.

200 shares @ $26 = $5,200 Cash Out
Covered Call writing premium of $2.38
$2.38 x 100 x 2 = $476 Cash In

200 shares @ $17.50 = $3,500 Cash Out
Covered Call writing premium of $1.50
$1.50 x 100 x 2 = $300 Cash In

200 shares @ $15 = $3,000 Cash Out
Covered Call writing premium of $1.25
$1.25 x 100 x 2 = $250 Cash In

200 shares @ $13.50 = $2,700 Cash Out
Covered Call writing premium of $1
$1 x 100 x 2 = $200 Cash In

Total Cash Out = $14,400
Total Cash In = $1,226 prior to expiration day

On expiration day, I sold all the shares—800—at their strike prices except for the $26 shares. They were sold at $21 each.

Let's re-cap:

200 at $13.50 = $2,700
200 at $15.00 = $3,000
200 at $17.50 = $3,500
200 at $21.00 = $4,200
Total proceeds at expiration day = $13,400

Add the $1,226 premiums I received to the total proceeds of the stock sale and I now had $14,626. This netted me $226 before commissions. Commissions were about $290 by the time this total transaction was complete. For me, this transaction came out positive even though it did not turn out the way I originally intended it to. My wife and I were on speaking terms at least.

Some stocks perform like teenagers; once you think you have figured them out, they do the opposite. It is extremely important for you to constantly study and restudy the basics. Know the resources that exist today in order to make educated decisions concerning the market.

Don't be scared to take a loss. If you can get out of your bad trades as early as possible, your good trades will have the space to thrive and increase. It's kind of like pruning trees. If you get rid of the bad, diseased, unhealthy parts of the tree, the plant then concentrates all of its growing energy on the more healthy, vibrant parts.

To limit your downside, use stop loss orders (not all brokers will do this). This is like a GTC order, but it generates an automatic sell if your position falls below a certain price. Let's say you purchase a stock at $10 per share. You can put in a stop loss order at $8. If the stock falls to $8, you are "stopped out," an order is generated to sell, and your loss has been capped.

Notes:

Don't go against the trend. If the trade is not doing what you want it to do, could your money be better used on another trade? Most of the time the answer is yes. There are more than enough profitable trades to invest in without wasting your time and money on unprofitable ones. If you have devised your game plan, then you know how your position should perform. If it is not performing, get out of the trade and go find one that will perform.

If your Simutrade account is taking a loss, there are only two reasons. First, you're not generating enough cash flow, or, second, your losing trades are eating all the increase. Take action now and include your exit strategies in your game plan. Don't let your profit get eaten by loss.

MONEY MANAGEMENT

Which do you think is safer, $10,000 in one trade or $10,000 in 10 trades with $1,000 per trade? Well, I hope you chose the smaller trade allocation. When we allocate all the resources at our disposal on one trade, we are risking everything. It could be great if that trade went well, but what would happen if some really bad news came out about the security behind our investment? Could we potentially lose a great percentage or maybe all of our money? You bet.

If you only have $1,000 invested in that same trade it takes a much smaller hit on the account. We may still have the same percentage, but it's only a percentage of $1,000, not that same percentage on $10,000.

If you are playing options, it's better to keep the total of all your strategy plays to fewer than 20% of your total portfolio amount. The majority, about 80%, should be invested in things like blue chip stocks, real estate, or other less risky investments.

Dividing the pie of your portfolio is a very common subject among brokerage houses and the stock market in general. I have seen a few different recommendations as to exactly what percentage of your assets should be in bonds, gold, stocks, options, et cetera. Just make sure that however you split your pie, the trades that are risking your money are less than 20% of your portfolio, maybe 30% if you have a very high tolerance for pain. The only exception to this is when you have a very small account. If you have $1,000 in an account, 20% would be $200. You might be limited in the trades that you do for $200. Are they out there? Yes, they most certainly are. You just have to look a little harder, that's all.

We need to make sure that we protect our assets. Too many people seem to concentrate on gain when they should be concentrating more on protecting what they have from loss. Live to trade another day. Cap your losses and let your profits run. Make sure that the money you put into your account stays in your account and multiplies. If you want to take out money to spend, take it out of your profits. Keep your principle amount safe so that it can continue to grow and work for you.

You need to diversify. Choose strategy candidates from different sectors or industries. If all of your open positions are in the oil sector and OPEC decides to create huge surpluses and drop out the bottom of oil prices, what will all your positions do? Go down. If you have only one or two positions in a sector that is decreasing, your other positions can still be on track and doing well.

Notes:

CHAPTER 7

The Simutrade System

Finally, we have arrived at the meat of this book—the Simutrade System. By now, you should have your Simutrade Game Plan Worksheet filled in and be ready to bolt out of the starting blocks. Follow the system outline below. Make sure to evaluate your trades and adjust your game plan if you don't get the results that you want.

Sometimes you'll find that certain concepts are more challenging to you. Capping your losses is one of the hardest for me. I constantly have to concentrate on getting out of my trades using my game plan criteria. If you find there are some skills that are difficult for you, divert more of your energy to mastering that skill. Seek out more information and hook up with a mentor or role model.

The Simutrade System is a working tool. Make it work for you. Milk it for all that you can and develop good decision making habits.

THE SIMUTRADE SYSTEM

1. Before you start trading:

   a. Complete the entire Simutrade Game Plan Worksheet. Make sure that the information necessary to make entry and exit decisions are included in your game plan.

Notes:

Notes:

2. Set up your brokerage account(s)

    a. Simutrade Account

        Fund your Simutrade account and decide on your method of tracking. You may use the Stock Transaction Tracking Record, or you may choose a spreadsheet, or portfolio tracking software. You may have a margin Simutrade account.

    b. Brokerage Account

        Your goal is to practice using the Simutrade System and then convert your Simutrading to real cash trades. Once you're ready, take the time to shop around for a good broker. This can save you loads of trouble and headaches. Make sure your brokerage account can trade options and consider getting a margin account.

THE DECISION MAKING PROCESS

Now that you have your account(s) all set up, and you have your game plan completed, you are ready for action. Let's take an overview of the process:

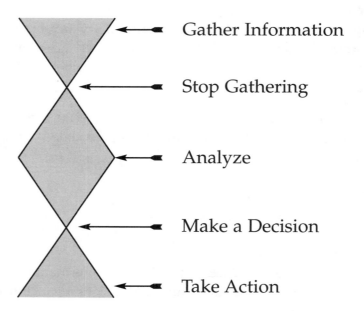

Gather Information

Stop Gathering

Analyze

Make a Decision

Take Action

I like this graphic. It represents simply the thought process this is used in the Simutrading System. Keep this graphic in mind as we continue.

GATHER INFORMATION

First, you must gather the information that you will need to make a good decision. That is what the Simutrade Worksheet is all about—getting the specific information that you need on each specific strategy. Practice being accurate and quick at collecting information.

You will find that you will be attracted to certain sources for information and will continually return to them when they prove useful. Try out W.I.N.™ (www.wadecook.com). You can find good candidates on almost every strategy at this one site. It is an excellent source for information. Try going on-line to get your quotes. The Chicago Board Options Exchange has an excellent website at www.cboe.com for getting quotes on a 20-minute delay, and it's *free*. Don't forget TeleChart 2000©'s search engine. You can search all tickers for certain criteria, like what stocks have just had a Peak or Slam.

Don't waste your time evaluating too much when you collect information. If you see a "red flag" (like volume under 50,000 or really bad P/E Ratio), stop collecting information. Move on to the next candidate.

It is to your benefit to have more than one candidate for the strategy you want to employ. Even though you may only want to purchase one Rolling Stock, find 10 and pick the best one. It's good to have something to compare, and you'll feel better about your decision.

EVALUATE AND PONDER

Now that you have collected information, stop and look over the Simutrade Worksheet. How does the chart look? Do you have at least three pluses (+++)? Is there a clear buy signal? Determine you exit point. Decide upon your targeted loss.

Can you get excited about this trade?

TAKE ACTION

You have two courses of action: 1) enter into the trade, and transfer the relevant information to your Tracking Record, or 2) don't enter the trade and move on the next worksheet.

This is Simutrading in a nutshell. The following is a detailed, systematic checklist for you to use as you Simutrade on your own.

1. Before you start trading:

   a. Complete the Game Plan Worksheet.

   b. Set up your Account(s)

      • Simutrade Account

      • Brokerage Account

2. Find a trade to originate.

   a. Locate eligible stock candidates.

   b. Review the strategy Step-By-Step Guide for candidates that fit the criteria.

      • Check the chart. Use the +/- system.

      • Gather the information on the Simutrade Worksheet, including P/E Ratio.

   c. Fill out the entire Simutrade Worksheet.

   d. Call your broker or get on-line and get current quotes.

3. Stop collecting information and evaluate the trade

   a. Check with your game plan to make sure the trade fits your criteria.

   b. Check for "Red Flags."

   c. Answer the questions: What is the the best use of my money? What is the best use of my time?

4. Take Action

   a. Act! Make your decision to enter into the trade.

      • Enter your trade into the Stock Transaction Tracking Record.

- Always write down your order. Make sure that you get into the habit of completing the Simutrade Worksheet, including the date, time, and broker/account. You may be glad that you have this information if you have any problems at your brokerage house. Your written notes are admissible in a court of law and can be used in any disputes.

b. Put ticker into watch list.

Don't Act. Move on to the next deal.

- Consider putting in watch list.

5. Daily (or periodic) routine

a. Check chart rating (+/-) for each open position.

b. Get a current quote.

c. Check for News.

d. Check against your game plan.

e. Decide:

- Everything looks okay. Stay in the trade, or

- Get out.

6. Monthly evaluations

Monthly (or any period of time that you determine) evaluations of your trades are extremely useful. This is how you test your game plan. Look at all the positions that you closed during the month. Have they performed like you expected? Are you on track with your game plan? Are you capping your losses adequately? Is your Return On Investment what it should be?

Evaluate all your open trades. Do you need to "clean house" and dump some losing trades to cap losses? Are you experiencing stress and maybe need to change your Time Temperament?

One good habit to keep things neat and tidy is to close out your transaction records monthly. This will allow simplification of record keeping. This also gives you an opportunity to review

Notes:

Notes:

each trade as you highlight it with a specific color and check your open trades as you carry them forward to the next month.

Here is one suggested use of the Simutrade Stock Transaction Tracking Record:

1. Check the accuracy of each transaction. Be sure to enter all details of the trade. This form is used as a daily record to document any and all transactions.

2. For easy reference, use a color coding system to see at a glance where you stand with each transaction:

    a. White or unmarked: Indicates this position is still open.

    b. Green: Indicates a closed position when results were positive. You can also use green when you hit your targeted loss. This is good, positive feedback because you have succeeded in capping your loss.

    c. Red: Indicates a closed position when results were negative.

    d. Blue: Indicates a position that was open and is transferred to the next month's record. This is still an open position (white) on next month's record.

Using the color coding makes your tracking records easy to evaluate. What color is predominately on each sheet? Do you have a lot of red? Why are those trades red? Do you have quite a few green highlights? If so, pat yourself on the back, you are on track.

The Simutrade System is fairly simple. Although it does depend upon what strategy that you use, Simutrading is generally quick and painless. I can spend less than half an hour evaluating all my open trades. The thing that takes the most time is finding and evaluating new trades. I enjoy the hunt, however, and would not mind spending a lot more time doing it.

Try this: Keep a rough estimate of the time that you spend using the Simutrade System. Then, divide that number by the profit that you have and see what your hourly wage is. I'll bet you'll be surprised.

The best advice I have concerning the Simutrade System is to use it. Try it out. Pick a strategy and do 10 trades. If you want to become an expert, do five trades each day. The more you use the Simutrade System, the greater the skill that you will acquire and the more potential you'll have for profit.

Notes:

THE
STRATEGIES

CHAPTER 8
Rolling Stocks

Rolling Stocks is a foundational strategy. I specifically use the word foundational for three reasons. 1) You can use the principles of Rolling Stocks and apply them to most other strategies. 2) They are simple enough to explain to a child, yet solid enough to create good cash flow and growth. 3) Rolling Stocks can provide part of a portfolio foundation—the bread-and-butter cash cow. You can receive excellent returns with relatively low risk.

The Rolling Stocks strategy has a long Time Temperament. A fast rolling stock may bounce from resistance to support in a month. This allows you more time to make good decisions and do accurate research. You don't have to feel rushed.

Rolling Stocks feel safe. You invest in the stocks of good solid companies. You know they are good solid companies because you check the fundamentals.

THE ROLLING STOCKS PERSON

If you were a "Rolling Stocks Person," you would probably do thorough research, check charts, draw lots and lots and lots of trendlines. You would search out and study fundamental analysis. These are important to Rolling Stocks. You may be holding this stock for awhile. You may roll the same stock over and over every few weeks or months, or sometimes years, mak-

Notes:

Notes:

ing a profit each time. If you want to be in for the long haul and make good solid returns, start with the fundamentals.

The term Rolling Stocks was devised by Wade Cook to describe the process of a stock that "channels" or "oscillates" between two price points—Resistance and Support. You purchase the stock when it is low (wholesale) and sell it when it is high (retail). You aren't out for a "killing." You just want to carve out a profit piece by piece. You might buy at $2 per share, then sell at $3 per share, purchase again at $2, and sell at $3. You may only roll from $1.06 to $1.47. Skeptics may disclaim, "Only a lousy 41¢? You should have seen my mutual fund move last year..." Just ask what their yield was. Then tell them yours.

I would love to get 41¢ all the time. Here's why: figure your yield. Cash In divided by Cash Out equals yield, which is also called Return On Investment. Let's say you buy a stock at $1.06 and you sell it at $1.47. Your Cash In of 41¢ divided by your Cash Out of $1.06 equals a Yield of 38%! In addition, it probably only took you two months. That's 19% a month. If you purchased 1,000 shares, you would pay $1,060 and receive $1,470.

Some people will balk and be frightened by what it would take to make 19% on a consistent basis. If a 19% rate of return is too high for you, just take some advice from me: "You can do twice as bad with your money; just make sure you do it on margin." Then you can live with only 10% a month, and laugh on your way to the bank.

Sometimes the hardest part of Rolling Stocks is to find stocks that are currently in a rolling range. *The Wall Street Journal* does not publish a list of "Rolling Stocks." You can not find a special screen on a pretty Bloomberg terminal, and there are but a handful of odd, miscellaneous references on the Internet. Therefore, you must learn the indicators so that you can find good Rolling Stocks on your own.

If this strategy interests you, I would suggest that you collect more information to gain a greater understanding. Pick up a copy of *Rolling Stock*, by Gregory Witt. It comprehensively explores Rolling Stocks aspects and will give you a solid knowledge base to get started right away with everything but experience. You can also read *Wall Street Money Machine* by the originator of Rolling Stocks, Wade Cook, or attend one of his seminars to get in touch with the best information on Rolling Stocks.

THE BASICS OF THE ROLLING STOCKS

First, you must find them. Search out a stock that channels in a consistent range. I know three ways to find Rolling Stocks.

1. Use a charting service and search. You can use a search engine or you can just scan through stocks and pick out the rolling pattern.

2. Get information off of W.I.N.™, at www.wadecook.com. They publish a list of potential stocks that are rolling on a periodic basis. Search the Internet and newsletters.

EXAMPLE FROM W.I.N.™:

7:52 AM PST

Research/Trading Department

Stocks under $5.00

Verity Inc. (VRTY) approximate range $4.50 - $5.50. Closed at $4^{7}/$_{16}$. Optionable.

Innovative Med Service (PURE) approximate range $1^{5}/$_{8}$ - $2^{5}/$_{8}$. Closed at $1^{11}/$_{16}$.

Gensia Sicor Inc. (GNSA) approximate range $4^{7}/$_{8}$ - $5^{7}/$_{8}$. Closed at $4^{15}/$_{16}$.

Today's Man Inc. (TMAN) approximate range $2^{7}/$_{8}$ - $3^{7}/$_{8}$. Closed at $3.

Senetek PLC (SNTKY) approximate range $4.00 - $5.00. Closed at $4^{1}/$_{16}$.

American International Petroleum Inc. (AIPN) approximate range $4.00 - $5.00. Closed at $4^{1}/$_{32}$.

Acclaim Entertainment (AKLM) approximate range $3.75 - $4.75. Closed at $3^{27}/$_{32}$. Optionable.

Quidel Corporation (QDEL) approximate range #3.00 - $4.00. Closed at $3³/₈.

7th Level (SEVL) approximate range $1.75 - $2.75. Closed at $1³/₄.

Stocks between $5.00 and $10.00

Imclone Systems Inc. (IMCL) approximate range $6.00 - $7.50. Closed at $6¹/₄. Optionable

Flanders Corporation (FLDR) approximate range $7.00 - $8.50. Closed at $7¹/₁₆.

L. L. Knickerbocker Company (KNIC) approximate range $6.00 - $7.50. Closed at $5¹³/₁₆.

Restrac Inc. (RTRK) approximate range $5.00 - $6.00. Closed at $5.00.

3. Find someone else who uses the Rolling Stocks strategy and compare notes. This could be a friend, a relative, or maybe even your broker.

Once you find a good source and can identify the chart pattern, it will seem easier.

The best candidates will be in a price range between 25¢ and $5. These lower priced stocks have a greater tendency to roll compared to stocks in a higher price range. Plus you will get a higher rate of return on a stock that rolls from $2 to $3 compared with a stock that rolls between $20 and $27. It may seem that the higher priced stock should be a better deal. Seven is still greater than one, is it not? Again, think in terms of your yield, and what is your money doing for you. Which is better, a 150% increase from $2 to $3, or 74% percent return from $20 to $27? Moreover, the roll between $2 and $3 allows you to have less money on the line, lowering your risk. You are increasing your leverage by using lower priced stocks. In addition, which do you think is easier, for a stock to move one point, or a stock to move seven points? I hope you see the simple yet powerful case in the positive favor of Rolling Stocks.

Once you collect five or 10 potential Rolling Stocks, get ready for the analysis. Find a straight edge, put it up to the chart, and draw support and resistance. Draw the trendline. If you're using TeleChart©, physically draw the trendline with your mouse. Remember not to be greedy. Draw more trendlines. You don't need to capture the whole height of the roll. You only need to capture a portion of the roll. After you have drawn a support and resistance line, stop, look at the chart, and ask yourself if you moved the lines together, could I get more rolls with a little smaller piece of the pie? Sometimes greed hits us and we try and squeeze the whole roll into our mouth. Greed is not your friend. Just concentrate on your small niblet of profit.

If you have identified support and resistance, you now have your entry and exit points. Purchase at support and sell at resistance. Make sure to calculate your yield and compare it to your game plan. If your target profit isn't on track with your game plan, then move on to another candidate.

Once you have all your contestant stocks dressed up with trendlines, fill out the Simutrade Worksheet. Look at the chart. Check the P/E Ratio, fundamentals, and rate the chart. Out of all the contestants, pick the best. You may find one, or you may find that they can all be good deals.

Now, stop collecting information.

Make a decision—either get in or move on.

Once you have found a Rolling Stock that fits your game plan, buy it, but not before you know your targeted profit and your stop loss. Directly after you buy, place a GTC order at your targeted exit point, probably the resistance trendline. When your sell order is filled in the future, watch the stock to return to support so that you can place another order to buy at your entry point. Use watch lists.

Once you feel comfortable with Rolling Stocks, it's time to use some Simutrades to gain confidence.

Notes:

Notes:

ROLLING STOCKS EXAMPLE 1

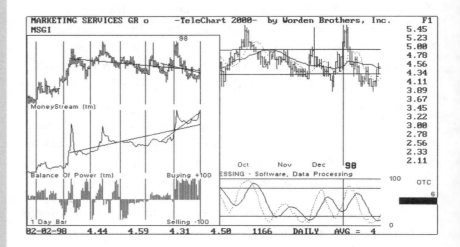

EVALUATION

Marketing Services (MSGI) has an awesome looking chart. We have a good roll between $4.30 and $5. We purchased 1,000 shares at $4¹/₂, and placed a GTC to sell at $5. On 2/11, the price fell below the moving average. On 2/12, the price was still below the moving average, so we sold on 2/12 for $4¹³/₃₂ for a loss of $100, or -2.1%. This is a successful trade because we have capped our losses. Look at what would have happened if we had ignored our moving averages and held on.

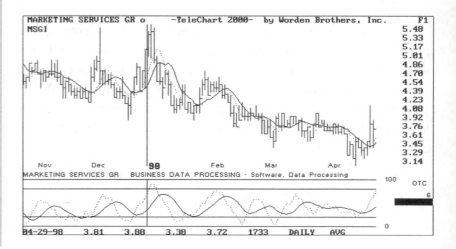

SIMUTRADE ROLLING STOCKS WORKSHEET

Date: 02/02/98 Time: 1:00 Broker: Simutrade

Company: Marketing Services Ticker: MSGI Quote: X $4¹/₂

Entry Point (Support Level): $4¹¹/₃₂ Exit Point (Resistance Level): $5

Shares Purchased: 1,000 Price: $4¹/₂

Notes: Good chart!

Associated GTCs placed: Sell 1,000 at $5

Closing Trade: 1,000 @ $4¹³/₃₂ Date: 02/12/98 Net Gain/Loss: -2.1%

Price Graph: +	Balance of Power™: +	**Note:**
Stochastics: +	Volume: +	*Never act upon less than a three plus (+++) or a three minus (- - -) chart.*
MoneyStream™: +	Trend: o	
Total score for this chart: ++++/+o		

Evaluation:

Cash Out: $4¹/₂ = $4.50 X 1,000 = $4,500.00

Cash In: $4¹³/₃₂ = $4.40625 X 1,000 = $4,406.25

$93.75 Loss

$93.75 / $4,500 = 2.1% Loss

Notes:

Notes:

ROLLING STOCKS EXAMPLE 2

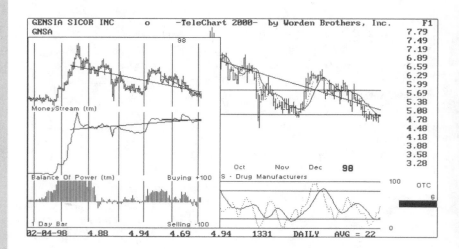

EVALUATION

GNSA has a good solid dollar roll and a (+++) chart. We've got a buy signal, but first let's target our profit. On my game plan, I have targeted a 15% profit for Rolling Stocks. Therefore, our entrance of $4^{15}/_{16}$ times 15% equals $5^{11}/_{16}$. The resistance is around $5^7/_8$, so we have a little room to play with. You may want to just target your support and resistance, and not have to calculate percentages. This would be okay. For me, and the examples in this book, my game plan targets specific yields.

We put in a GTC order to sell 1,000 at $5^{11}/_{16}$. We were filled on 2/12/98 with a net gain of $750 or a yield of 15.19%.

SIMUTRADE ROLLING STOCKS WORKSHEET

Date: 02/04/98   Time: 1:00   Broker: Simutrade

Company: Gensia, Inc.   Ticker: GNSA   Quote: X $4^{15}/$_{16}$

Entry Point (Support Level): $4^7/$_8$ Exit Point (Resistance Level): $5^7/$_8$

Shares Purchased: 1,000   Price: $4^{15}/$_{16}$

Notes: Good chart! Target Profit @ 15% = $5^{11}/$_{16}$

Associated GTCs placed: Sell 1,000 at $5^{11}/$_{16}$

Closing Trade: 1,000 @ $5^{11}/$_{16}$ Date: 02/12/98   Net Gain/Loss: 15.19%

Price Graph: +   Balance of Power™: +

Stochastics: +   Volume: +

MoneyStream™: o   Trend: o

Total score for this chart: +++o/+o

Note:
Never act upon less than a three plus (+++) or a three minus (- - -) chart.

Evaluation:

Cash Out:	$4^{15}/$_{16}$	= $4.9375	X 1,000 =	$4,937.50
Cash In:	$5^{11}/$_{16}$	= $5.5875	X 1,000 =	$5,687.50
				$750.00 Gain

$750 / $4,937.50 = 15.19% Gain

Notes:

ROLLING OPTION EXAMPLE 1

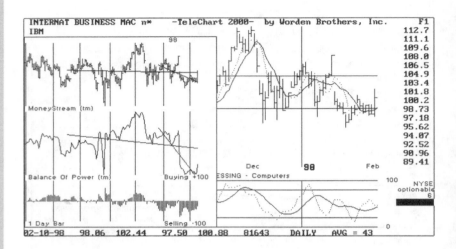

EVALUATION

I found a great chart while looking at IBM. It had a nice, consistent roll between about $99 and $105. I did not, however, have the cash to buy $100,000 worth of stock in one play. So, I turned this into a Rolling Option. The strategy is the same, except you purchase a Call Option instead of the stock.

I purchase 10 March $100 Calls for $5. My Cash Out was $5,000. I calculated my 25% profit and put a GTC order to sell at $6¹/₄. I was filled on 2/25/98 with a cash gain of $1,250.

Remember not to rule out a trade because you don't have enough money until you check out the options.

SIMUTRADE BUYING CALLS WORKSHEET

Date: 02/10/98   Time: 1:00   Broker: Simutrade

Company: IBM   Ticker: IBM   Quote: _____ X 100^7/_8$

P/E: _____   News: None

Notes: Price too high for Rolling Stocks. Play Rolling Option. Buy calls at $99, sell at $104.

Option: Mar $100 Call   Option Ticker: _____   Quote: _____ X $5

Contracts Purchased: 10   Price: $5

Exit Strategy: 25%   5 X 1.25 = 6^1/_4$

Associated GTCs placed: Sell 10 Mar $100 C @ 6^1/_4$

Closing Trade: 10 @ 6^1/_4$ Date: 02/25/98   Net Gain/Loss: 25%

Price Graph: +	Balance of Power™: o	**Note:**
Stochastics: o	Volume: +	*Never act upon less*
MoneyStream™: +	Trend: +	*than a three plus (+++)*
Total score for this chart: +o+o/++		*or a three minus (- - -)*
		chart.

Evaluation: _____

Cash Out:	$5	= $5	X 1,000 =	$5,000
Cash In:	6^1/_4$	= $6.25	X 1,000 =	$6,250
				$1,250 Gain

$1,250 / $5,000 = 25% Gain

Notes:

| | OPEN | | | | | | | | | | CLOSE | | | | |
Date	Stock	Price	B/S	Qty	Position	O/C	Ord	Fill $	Total	Date	B/S	Qty	Fill $	Total	Comms
2/2	MSGI	$4^1/_2$	B	1000	Long		1	$4^1/_2$	4,500	2/12	S	1000	$4^{13}/_{32}$	4,406	
Strategy	Rolling Stocks			Notes						P/L $ -93.75			Days 10	Yield	-2.1 %
2/4	GNSA	$4^{15}/_{16}$	B	1000	Long		2	$4^{15}/_{16}$	4,937.50	2/12	S	1000	$5^{11}/_{16}$	5,687.50	
Strategy	Rolling Stocks			Notes						P/L $ 750			Days 8	Yield	15.19 %
2/10	IBM	$100^7/_8$	B	10	Mar 100 C		1	5	5,000	2/25	S	10	$6^1/_4$	6,250	
Strategy	Rolling Option			Notes						P/L $ 1,250			Days 15	Yield	25 %
Strategy				Notes						P/L $			Days	Yield	%
Strategy				Notes						P/L $			Days	Yield	%
Strategy				Notes						P/L $			Days	Yield	%
Strategy				Notes						P/L $			Days	Yield	%
Strategy				Notes						P/L $			Days	Yield	%
Strategy				Notes						P/L $			Days	Yield	%

CHAPTER 9
Buying Calls And Puts

There are several reasons for investing in options, but the main reason is as Wade Cook has stated,

> "When there is a small movement in the stock, there is a magnified movement in the option."

Remember, however, *options are very risky!* Be sure your portfolios are well allotted with other plays. If I buy Calls or Puts in my portfolio, I try to use the 80/20 rule. That is, 80% of my portfolio is in the low risk arena and the other 20% is in higher risk area. This diversification can lessen my amount of risk and exposure.

I learned this concept by sad experience. By the time that I finally figured out not to spend all of my money on options all at once, I had lost some money. Fortunately for me, a portion of the money I lost was in my Simutrade account. I simply went back to the basics to do more lay ups, fine tune my game plan, and get back on track.

When we buy either a Call or a Put, we want to make a profit. We generally are not interested in owning the stock; we just want the magnified movement of the option price to return to us our little piece of profit. Remember that we must play the strategy, not the stock. We want to locate and purchase a stock or option that will go up in value so that we may sell at a profit. That is the strategy.

Notes:

Notes:

When you buy a Call on a stock, you think the stock is going to increase in value. You want the stock to go up in price. Remember the definition: An option is the right, *not the obligation,* to purchase a stock at a certain price on a certain day. I recommend you surf the charts. You are looking for a good, positive chart with a trend pattern going up. Use all of the parameters on the Simutrade Worksheet for analyzing the details of charts and make effective decisions.

When you buy a Put, it is exactly the same as buying a Call except you think that the stock is going to decrease in value. You want a negative chart with a trend showing the stock going in a downward direction.

These two important strategies are the basic building blocks of all the other options strategies. It is extremely important in your progression of becoming an expert in Calls and Puts to study the basics. Use the Simutrade System to perfect your skills and understanding of these strategies.

Let's look at some examples and analyze the strategies.

BUYING CALLS EXAMPLE 1

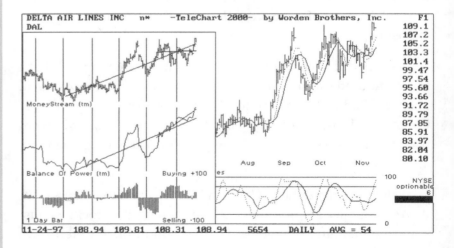

EVALUATION

I purchased 10 December $110 Calls on DAL for $3³/₄. That's a Cash Out of $3,750. I calculated a target profit of 25% and placed a GTC order to sell all 10 contracts at $4¹¹/₁₆. My GTC order was filled on 12/1 for a successful profit of $937.50.

Looking back on the trade, I could have targeted more profit. My options were above $10 on December 10th, just nine days later. Don't get greedy. I'm happy with 25%. You must determine your own target profit and stick to it. Follow your game plan.

SIMUTRADE BUYING CALLS WORKSHEET

Date: __11/24/97__ Time: __1:00__   Broker: __Simutrade__

Company: __Delta Airlines__   Ticker: __DAL__ Quote: _____ X $108¹⁵/₁₆

P/E: _____   News: __None__

Notes: __Good buy signal.__

Option: __Dec $110 Call__   Option Ticker: _____   Quote: _____ X $3³/₄

Contracts Purchased: __10__   Price: __$3³/₄__

Exit Strategy: ____25%   3.75 X 1.25 = 4.6875 = $4¹¹/₁₆____

Associated GTCs placed: __Sell 10 Dec $110 C @ $4¹¹/₁₆__

Closing Trade: __10 @ $4¹¹/₁₆__ Date: __12/01/97__ Net Gain/Loss: __25%__

Price Graph: ___-___	Balance of Power™: ___+___	**Note:**
Stochastics: ___o___	Volume: ___+___	*Never act upon less than a three plus (+++) or a three minus (- - -) chart.*
MoneyStream™: ___+___	Trend: ___+___	
Total score for this chart: __-o++/++__		

Evaluation: _____

Cash Out:	$3³/₄	= $3.75	X 1,000 = $3,750
Cash In:	$4¹¹/₁₆	= $4.6875	X 1,000 = $4,687.50
			$937.50 Gain

$937.50 / $3,750 = 25% Gain

BUYING CALLS EXAMPLE 2

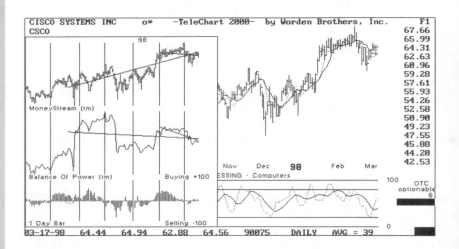

EVALUATION

Here is a chart giving us an okay buy signal. The moving averages have just crossed and are heading up, and so are the stochastics. I purchased 10 contracts of the April $65 Calls at $3⁷/₈. My target of 25% is $4²⁷/₃₂; I place a GTC to sell all 10. On the 24th, the option took a nice jump up, but not quite enough to give me a fill. Then, on the 25th, the price of the option opened above $5, there was a gap. Since I usually review the charts in the morning, I put in an order to sell at $5¹/₂, and canceled my GTC. I was filled at $5¹/₂, giving me a profit of $1,625 or 41.9%.

SIMUTRADE BUYING CALLS WORKSHEET

Date: 03/17/98   Time: 1:00   Broker: Simutrade

Company: Cisco Systems   Ticker: CSCO   Quote: _____ X $64^9/₁₆

P/E: _____   News: None

Notes: _____

Option: Apr $65 Call   Option Ticker: _____   Quote: _____ X $3^7/₈

Contracts Purchased: 10   Price: $3^7/₈

Exit Strategy: 25% 3^7/₈ = 3.875 X 1.25 = 4.84375 = $4^{27}/₃₂

Associated GTCs placed: Sell 10 Apr $65 C @ $4^{27}/₃₂

Closing Trade: 10 @ $5^1/₂   Date: 03/25/98   Net Gain/Loss: 41.9%

		Note:
Price Graph: +	Balance of Power™: o	*Never act upon less*
Stochastics: +	Volume: +	*than a three plus (+++)*
MoneyStream™: +	Trend: +	*or a three minus (- - -)*
Total score for this chart: +++o/++		*chart.*

Evaluation: _____

Cash Out:	$3^7/₈	= $3.875	X 1,000 = $3,875
Cash In:	$5^1/₂	= $5.50	X 1,000 = $5,500
			$1,625 Gain

$1,625 / $3,875 = 41.9% Gain

Notes:

BUYING PUTS EXAMPLE 1

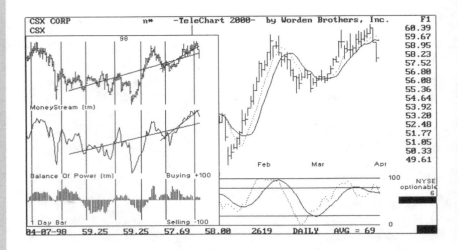

EVALUATION

The chart of CSX is a negative chart. Remember, we are buying Puts. I purchased 10 May $55 Puts at $5/8. My target was $5/8 plus 25%. I put in an order to sell all 10 contracts at $7/8. On 4/15 I was filled with a profit of $250. When I calculated my gain percentage, it came out to 40%. This was an error on my part on calculating the target profit. I was trying to round up to 25% and rounded up too much. All in all, I was glad that I made the error. I made a 40% return.

SIMUTRADE BUYING PUTS WORKSHEET

Date: __04/07/98__ Time: ___1:00___ Broker: ___Simutrade___

Company: __Csx Corporation__ Ticker: __CSX__ Quote: _____ X _$58_

P/E: _____ News: ___None___

Notes: _____

Option: __May $55 Put__ Option Ticker: _____ Quote: _____ X $$^5/_8$

Contracts Purchased: ___10___ Price: ___$$^5/_8$

Exit Strategy: ____25% $$^5/_8$ = .625 X 1.25 = .875 = $$^7/_8$

Associated GTCs placed: __Sell 10 May $55 C @ $$^7/_8$

Closing Trade: _10 @ $$^7/_8$__ Date: _04/15/98_ Net Gain/Loss: ___40%

Price Graph: ___-___	Balance of Power™: __0__	**Note:**
Stochastics: ___-___	Volume: _____+___	*Never act upon less*
MoneyStream™: _-_	Trend: _____-___	*than a three plus (+++)*
Total score for this chart: __- - - 0/+ -__		*or a three minus (- - -)*
		chart.

Evaluation: _____

Cash Out:	$$^5/_8$	= $.625	X 1,000 =	$625
Cash In:	$$^7/_8$	= $.875	X 1,000 =	$875
				$250 Gain

$250 / $625 = 40% Gain

Notes:

STOCK TRANSACTION TRACKING RECORD

| | OPEN | | | | | | | | | | CLOSE | | | | |
Date	Stock	Price	B/S	Qty	Position	O/C	Ord Fill $	Total		Date	B/S	Qty	Fill $	Total	Comms
11/24	DAL	108$^{15}/_{16}$	B	10	Dec 110 C	1	3$^3/_4$	3,750		12/1	S	10	4$^{11}/_{32}$	4,687.50	
Strategy Buy Call					Notes					P/L $ 937.50			Days 7	Yield	25%
3/17	CSCO	64$^9/_{16}$	B	10	Apr 65 C	2	3$^7/_8$	3,875		3/25	S	10	5$^1/_2$	5,500	
Strategy Buy Call					Notes					P/L $ 1,625			Days 8	Yield	41.9%
4/17	CSX	58	B	10	May 55 P	1	$^5/_8$	625		4/15	S	10	$^7/_8$	875	
Strategy Buy Put					Notes					P/L $ 250			Days 8	Yield	40%
										P/L $			Days	Yield	%
Strategy					Notes										
										P/L $			Days	Yield	%
Strategy					Notes										
										P/L $			Days	Yield	%
Strategy					Notes										
										P/L $			Days	Yield	%
Strategy					Notes										
										P/L $			Days	Yield	%
Strategy					Notes										
										P/L $			Days	Yield	%
Strategy					Notes										

CHAPTER 10
Writing Covered Calls

The strategy of Writing Covered Calls is probably one of the safest, easiest methods to enter into the Stock Market. "Writing" a Covered Call is the lingo for selling a Covered Call. Plus, with Writing Covered Calls you can be paid twice (and maybe more) on the same investment. With two ways to win, this strategy can be an excellent cash flow builder.

Writing Covered Calls blends the elements of buying stocks and using options. This blend allows you to own stock and charge "rent" for it.

WHERE TO FIND COVERED CALLS TO WRITE

Covered Call candidates are relatively easy to find. Probably just because of the sheer number of applicants, Covered Calls can be found all over. Just look for stocks whose price is from $5 to $25, optionable (you are able to trade options on this stock), and a little volatile—going up and down. Then evaluate the trade using the Simutrade Covered Call Worksheet.

When stocks are below $5, there are generally no options available. You cannot buy or sell options because there is no "product." Stocks that are above $5 generally have options available. You can buy and sell puts and calls.

Notes:

You want to keep the current price under $25 per share because you have to be "covered"—or you need to have purchased the stock—for this strategy. One thousand shares at $25 equal $25,000. Not exactly pocket change for most people.

Excellent sources for finding Covered Call candidates are the Wealth Information Network™ (W.I.N.™), newspapers, and the Internet in general. Go purchase a *Wall Street Journal*. Look under the Listed Options Quotations section. A quick rule of thumb when you look at the quotation page is to target a Covered Call with 10% yield from the premium. If you find a $10 stock, you need a $1 premium. If you find a $15 stock, make sure that you can get $1^1/$_2$ in premiums for writing the call.

For our example candidates, I looked up a day on W.I.N.™, printed out the Potential Covered Calls list, and viewed all the tickers on TeleChart 2000©. W.I.N.™ has a list of Potential Covered Calls quite often. Here are three examples:

February 9, 1998

8:40 AM PST

POTENTIAL COVERED CALLS:

PICTURETEL CORPORATION (PCTL) is trading around $7^9/$_{16}$. The March $7.50 calls are trading around $^{13}/$_{16}$. This could be a 21.49% return, and if you are called out, it could be a 19.83% return.

PLC SYSTEMS INC. (PLC) is trading around $11^{11}/$_{16}$. The March $12.50 calls are trading around $1^1/$_{16}$. This could be an 18.18% return, and if you are called out, it could be a 32.09% return.

TRUMP HOTELS (DJT) is trading around $11^9/$_{16}$. The March $12.50 calls are trading around $1. This could be a 17.30% return, and if you are called out, it could be a 33.51% return.

The term "Writing Covered Calls" has three words that describe the aspects of the strategy.

"Covered" means that you own the underlying security on a derivative. A call is an option, and an option is a type of a derivative—you do not buy the stock, but a contract for that stock. Basically, if you are "covered," you own the stock that you are selling the right for someone else to buy from you.

A simpler explanation would be to say that you are covered if you own the stock that the option is written for. You own the stock, therefore your option is covered. You are using the stock as collateral for the call.

What is the meaning of "Writing?" Think of writing as originating. You are the source. You can buy an option contract without writing it. Remember the definition for an option? The right, not the obligation, to purchase a stock at a specific strike price on or before a particular expiration date. Well, when you write an option, things change just a little. You now have taken on some responsibility and receive a premium for doing so. You now have the obligation to perform on the contract you are writing if your options are exercised before the option expires. When you are writing a call, you are selling someone the option to buy the stock from you at the strike price. When that someone who has purchased your option exercises his right to "call your stock away" you get "called out" you have the obligation to sell the stock at your strike price.

Since you may get your stock called away from you, would it not be prudent to make sure you would make money if this event took place? Here's the answer: When you write your call, make sure it is for the next higher strike price. There are two reasons for this. One is a capital gain. You want capital gains. The key word there is "gain." If I purchase a stock at $9 a share, I want to be able to sell it at a higher price. I need to be in the business of making a profit. I would choose a strike price on my option of $10. If you could know for certain that you could purchase a stock at $9 and then know exactly when you could sell it at $10, would you do it? That's what Writing Covered Calls is all about. That's what I just did.

Also, since your main goal is to create cash flow from receiving premiums, you'll want to pick an option with an expiration of the next month out. You want your money back as soon as possible. If you are nearing the next expiration day, the third Friday of each month, then you may choose to extend your play one more month based upon receiving more premium for more time value. This can increase your yield and create a more regular cash flow.

So, the target strategy of Writing Covered Calls would be to purchase a stock in 100 share increments (each Call Option is a contract for 100 shares). Then, write a call for the next higher strike price that expires in less than two months, usually less than 30 days.

The key to choosing which Covered Call is good to write is by the yield. Sometime in the very beginning of your candidate search, stop and calculate yield. Do this for each candidate. Narrow your candidates down to 5 or 10 that you like based upon the yield.

The formula for yield is:

Cash In (CI)/Cash Out (CO) = Yield

The formula for Writing a Covered Call when you get called out is:

CI (premiums)+CI (capital gains)/Cash Out (stock)= Yield

If you don't get called out, then just drop off the capital gains like this:

CI (premiums)/Cash Out(stock) = Yield

Make sure your candidates match your game plan. Look up and evaluate each chart (+++ or greater). Use the Simutrade Worksheet to help you gather the information.

I like to run through examples because then I can see and feel how this works. Then I can have the terms fit into their proper place and grasp them easier.

For my example, I find a stock that is in my price range and optionable. I make sure it has a good chart. My example candidate company, ticker symbol ZYX is currently trading at bid: $9^1/$_4$ x ask: $9^1/$_2$. I purchase 1,000 shares for $9,500 (9^1/$_2$ = 9.5 x 1,000 shares = 9,500). I now own 1,000 shares of ZYX.

The next step is to Write a Call for the next month and the next higher strike price. Let's assume it is the first part of April. Therefore, I would choose the April $10 Call on ZYX. I check the price for the April $10 Call and it is trading at $1 x $1^1/$_4$. I Write a Covered Call and receive $1 per share. Since I own 1,000 shares, I can write 10 contracts (one contract equals 100 shares). That's $1,000 in premium, in my account and in cold hard cash. That's a yield of over 10.5%. Nevertheless, I'm not done yet. What happens if I get called out?

Remember that I still own the stock and have an obligation or responsibility. If, on the expiration day, the price of the stock is higher than my strike price, someone could exercise their option to buy my stock at $10 per share. They could then go out into the market and sell it at a higher price. I may be called out. If I am called out, I am obligated to sell my stock at $10 per share. I purchased the stock at $9^1/$_2$ and was called out, or sold it, at $10. My position is closed. Therefore, I make an additional 50¢ per share, or $500 in capital gains. This increases my yield to over 15% ($1,000 CI + $500 CI/$9,500 CO = 15.8%). Not bad. I invested $9,500 and got back $11,000. I just made $1,500.

Oh, but I forgot, I did this trade in my Simutrade margin account. Now, calculate what would happen. The math is simple—multiply your yield by two (assume 50% margin) and you've just made 31% on your money. Let's see if we can have a short recap of our trade so far.

1. We no longer own the stock.

2. We have fulfilled our obligation as a Covered Call Writer.

3. We have our initial investment of $9,500.

4. We made a profit of $1,500 ($1,000 for the writing premium and $500 from being called out).

5. We had a profit of over 15% (over 30% if on margin).

Notes:

Notes:

Not too shabby. But wait, there is one more element. What do we do if we are not exercised? We get to keep our $1,000 premium and we still own the stock after the expiration date.

First, let's go to the expiration date, which is the third Saturday of every month. Since we can't trade on the weekends, it follows that the crucial day for determining if we are "called out" of our options would be the Friday before. In our example above, what would we do if, on the expiration date, we were not called out? We would still own the stock. Probably, the price of the stock did not rise above $10, otherwise we would have had a higher chance of being called out.

You could sell the stock for $9 and make a profit. Wait, didn't we buy the stock at 9^1/_2$? If so, how can we make a profit at $9? Cost Basis. We purchased the stock for $9.50. We received a premium of $1,000, or $1 per share. That lowers our cost basis to $8.50. It's like we just purchased the stock at $8.50 instead of buying at $9.50 and Writing a Call for $1. It's just like receiving rent for owning stock. Isn't rent usually monthly?

Well, why not write another Covered Call for the next month out and receive another premium? Another rent check. If you did this each month for a year, what would be your cost basis? It would be just like someone paid for stock, gave you the stock, and then paid you extra money, just because. This would keep your money working.

By the way, statistics show that only about 15% of all the Covered Calls that you write will be exercised. You may be able to write call after call after call on the same stock. Do you think you can generate monthly cash flow from just a couple Covered Calls? You bet!

There is one other scenario that you need to be aware of. What happens if you write a Covered Call and the price of the stock goes down or takes a dive? We probably won't get called out because someone could go into the market and purchase shares at a lower price compared to our stock price. Remember though, we still own the stock. If the stock price is going down, so is the value of our Covered Call. Let me ask you a question. What do you think the value of the option is doing? Going down? You bet. Why not just buy back calls at a lower price and close our position out. We may have to give up some of our profits, but I'd rather have a smaller profit than any loss. Slick exit, huh? Could you put this little scenario into your game plan? I would.

Let's look at some filled out Simutrades and a chart for the W.I.N.™ examples that we used earlier in this chapter.

Notes:

Notes:

WRITING COVERED CALLS EXAMPLE 1

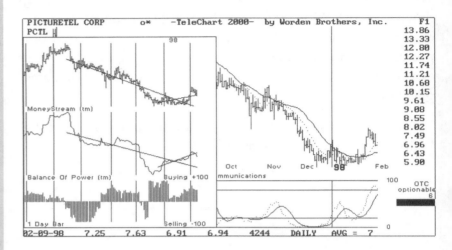

EVALUATION

This is a candidate I found on W.I.N.™ After looking at the chart, I purchased 1,000 shares at $7⁹/₁₆ for a Cash Out of $7,562.50. I then wrote a March $7.50 call and received a premium of $¹³/₁₆. This is 10.7% return.

On the expiration date, I did not get called out. I still own the stock. At this time, I looked at the chart again to determine if I wanted to sell the stock or write another call. In this particular case, I chose to write another call. That, however, is another trade.

Notes:

SIMUTRADE COVERED CALLS WORKSHEET

Date: 02/09/98   Time: 1:00   Broker: Simutrade

Company: Picturetel Corporation   Ticker: PCTL   Quote: X $7⁹/₁₆

P/E: _____   News: From WIN

Notes: If not called out, write for next month

Option: Mar $7¹/₂ Call   Option Ticker: _____   Quote: X $¹⁵/₁₆

Shares Purchased: 1,000   Price: $7⁹/₁₆

Contracts Sold: 10 Mar $7¹/₂ Call   Price: $¹⁵/₁₆

Associated GTCs placed: _____

Closing Trade: Expired   Date: 03/20/98   Net Gain/Loss: 10.7%

Price Graph: __-__   Balance of Power™: __+__

Stochastics: __-__   Volume: __+__

MoneyStream™: __-__   Trend: __+__

Total score for this chart: __- - - +/++__

Note:
Never act upon less than a three plus (+++) or a three minus (- - -) chart.

Evaluation: _____

Cash Out:	$7⁹/₁₆	=	$7.5625	X 1,000 = $7,652.50
Cash In: (Premium)	$¹⁵/₁₆	=	$.812.50	X 1,000 = $1,062.50
Cash In: (Stock)				

$812.50 Gain

$812.50 / $7,652.50 = 10.7% Gain

Margin: $812.50 / $3,781.25 = 21.5% Gain

Notes:

WRITING COVERED CALLS EXAMPLE 2

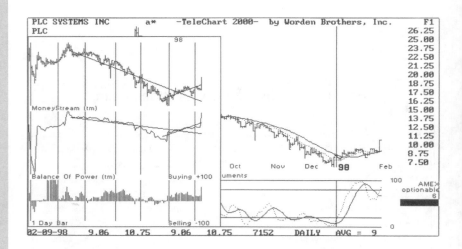

EVALUATION

This Covered Call was also found on W.I.N.™ I like the candidates that they list in their Covered Call list. I purchased the stock at $11^{11}/_{16}$ for a Cash Out of $11,687.50. Then I wrote a March $12.50 call and received a premium of $1^{1}/_{16}$, or $1,062.50. This is a 9.1% return. On the ex-date, I was called out of my 1,000 shares for my strike price of $12.50. This gave me an additional 6.9% return, for a total of under 16%.

SIMUTRADE COVERED CALLS WORKSHEET

Date: _02/09/98_   Time: ____1:00____   Broker: _____Simutrade_____

Company: _PLC Systems Inc_____   Ticker: _PLC_   Quote: _____ X _$11$¹¹/₁₆

P/E: _____   News: _From WIN_____

Notes: _If not called out, write for next month_____

Option: _Mar 12^{1}/₂ Call_____   Option Ticker: _____   Quote: _____ X 1^{1}/₁₆

Shares Purchased: ___1,000_____   Price: _$11$¹¹/₁₆_____

Contracts Sold: _10 Mar 12^{1}/₂ Call_____   Price: _1^{1}/₁₆_____

Associated GTCs placed: _____

Closing Trade: _1,000 @ 12^{1}/₂_ Date: _03/20/98___ Net Gain/Loss: ____16%____

Price Graph: ____+____ Balance of Power™: ___+___		**Note:**
Stochastics: ____o____ Volume: _____ +		*Never act upon less*
MoneyStream™: _+_ Trend: _____ +		*than a three plus (+++)*
Total score for this chart: _+o++/++_		*or a three minus (- - -)*
		chart.

Evaluation: _____

  Cash Out: $11$¹¹/₁₆   = $11.6875   X 1,000 = $11,687.50

  Cash In: (Premium) 1^{1}/₁₆   = $1.0625   X 1,000 = $1,062.50

  Cash In: (Stock) 12^{1}/₂   = $12.50   X 1,000 = $12,500.00

                                                $1,875.00 Gain

  $1,875 / $11,687.50 = 16% Gain

  Margin: $1,875 / $5,843.75 = 32% Gain

Notes:

STOCK TRANSACTION TRACKING RECORD

	OPEN									CLOSE					
Date	Stock	Price	B/S	Qty	Position	O/C	Ord	Fill $	Total	Date	B/S	Qty	Fill $	Total	Comms
2/9	PCTL	7 9/16	B	1000	Long		1	7 9/16	7,652.50						
Strategy				Notes				P/L $					Days	Yield	%
			S	10	Mar 7.5 C		1a	13/16	812.50						
Strategy Covered Call				Notes				P/L $	812.50				Days 29	Yield	10.7 %
2/9	PCL	11 11/16	B	1000	Long		2	11 11/16	11,687.50	3/20	S	1000	12 1/2	12,500	
Strategy				Notes				P/L $					Days	Yield	%
			S	10	Mar 12.5 C		2a	1 1/16	1,062.50						
Strategy Covered Call				Notes				P/L $	1,875				Days 29	Yield	16 %
Strategy				Notes				P/L $					Days	Yield	%
Strategy				Notes				P/L $					Days	Yield	%
Strategy				Notes				P/L $					Days	Yield	%
Strategy				Notes				P/L $					Days	Yield	%
Strategy				Notes				P/L $					Days	Yield	%

CHAPTER 11

Stock Splits

The Stock Splits strategy offers high gain in a short time frame. It is not uncommon to make 25, 50, or 100% or more in a matter of weeks or days. Stock Splits are high risk scenarios because of their volatility. To reduce risk, I use timing as an extremely important parameter to achieve successful Simutrades.

When a stock splits, it literally does just that—one share becomes two (or more) shares. The most common split ratio is 2:1. That means that if you had 100 shares of stock before the split date, you would have 200 shares after the split date. In essence, you have doubled the amount of shares that you own. The price of the stock also splits. If your 100 shares had a price of $80 before the split, you would have 200 shares at $40 after the split.

Although the most common split ratio is 2:1, other ratios abound. There are 3:1, 4:1, and even 10:1. There are odd splits like 5:4, 3:2. You can have successful trades with any of the split ratios, but the more shares you get, the greater probability of making a profit when they go up in price.

After a stock splits, the price of many stocks have a tendency to go back to the original price before the split occurred, especially with good companies with good revenues. This means that our 100 shares at $80 splits to 200 shares at $40 and will

Notes:

Notes:

have a tendency to increase in price back up to $80 again. Does this happen every time? No. It does happen often. This puts the odds in our favor and it's good to have the odds in your favor.

There are at least five entry points and time frames to exercise the Stock Split strategy. This equates to greater versatility within the same strategy. Multiple variations of the Stock Split strategy are possible on one split. Let's address all five entry points, one at a time, in the general sequence which they occur.

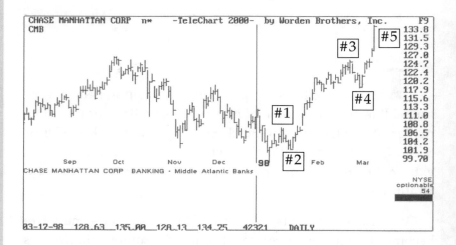

THE FIVE ENTRY POINTS

ENTRY POINT 1: HISTORICAL ANALYSIS

Company's stocks tend to split on a historical trend and follow certain patterns. If you can find a stock that splits on a regular basis, say every year or two, and confirm certain indicators or clues, you may be able to jump in before the split is actually announced. To see this, look at DELL, LLY, and PFE.

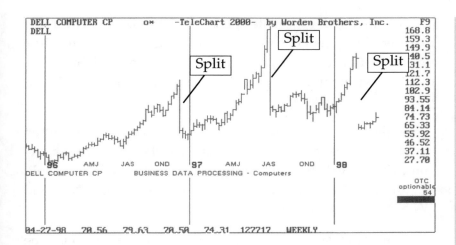

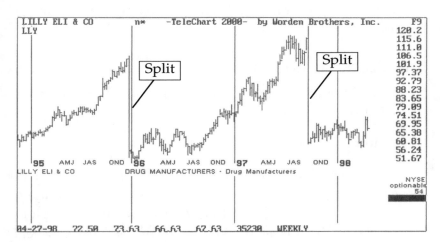

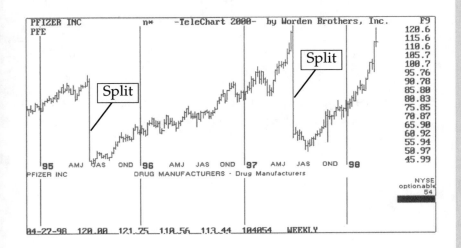

Potential split candidates generally leave certain clues that experienced traders like to follow. Although it may take a little time and effort on your part, the signals that a Stock Split candidate leave are unique and easy to spot and make a good footprint.

Some like to call this first entry point "getting in on rumors." The old adage "buy on rumor, sell on announcement" comes into play here. In actuality, reliable rumors of a stock split are often tradable. Information sources like CNBC, FNN, and W.I.N.™, are vital to get in on rumors.

A rumor means that the experienced traders are noticing the clues and acting on them. Is it good to follow experts? Yes, it usually is.

THE CLUES TO LOOK FOR

We've already mentioned rumors. This is one of four major clues that surface. Here is a short list:

1. Rumors. These should be from reliable sources.

2. Annual shareholders meeting or Board of Directors meetings. Usually the company has to authorize more shares in order to split stock. The Board of Directors makes this decision. When a Board of Directors gets together, things usually happen, so check for other kinds of news also.

3. Shareholders receive a notice to increase the number of shares, usually by 50 to 100%.

4. Price Gaps. Gaps in price can often indicate news leaks and insider trading before the announcement is made to the general public.

STOCK SPLITS EXAMPLE 1

On February 17, 1998, I was casually talking about my paper trading to a qualified individual. I was getting the evaluation of some of my trades by someone that I felt had much more experience and knowledge than I. As I was talking to him he mention to me that I ought to check out Lucent Technologies and Dell Computer. The rumor on CNBC was that both stocks were going to announce a split, possibly the next day. This went right along with my game plan, so I decided to do so.

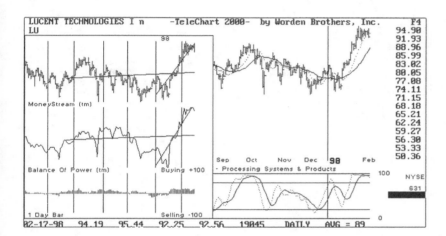

I double checked with W.I.N.™ (it was also on IQ Pager™), and sure enough, there was Lucent.

February 17, 1998

12:37 PM PST

Trading/Research Department Update

We placed an order for Lucent Technologies (LU) calls today based on the news that Lucent will have a Board of Directors meeting tomorrow. We are playing the possibility of a split announcement—this is split entry point #1, the pre-announcement trade. The April $90 calls were trading at $6⁷/₈ x $7¹/₄. Our order was to buy 10 contracts at $7 or better, good for the day, and we got our fill at $7. We are waiting to place a GTC to sell to see if they announce a split in the near future.

Notes:

SIMUTRADE STOCK SPLITS WORKSHEET

Strategy: ____Preannouncement_____
     (Preannouncement, Announcement, Post Announcement, DUCk, et cetera)

Date: _02/17/98_ Time: __1:00_____ Broker: _Simutrade_____

Company: _Lucent Technologies_____ Ticker: _LU____ Quote: _____ X 86^9/_{32}$

Split Date: _____ Split Ratio: _____

Option: _Apr $90 Call___ Option Ticker: _LUCR_____ Quote: _____ X 5^5/_8$

Notes: _Watch every day for exits._____

Contracts Purchased: ___10_____   Price: _5^5/_8$_____

Exit Strategy: __Target: 25 - 100%_____

Associated GTCs placed: _____

Closing Trade: _10 @ 11^5/_8$_ Date: _02/19/98__ Net Gain/Loss: ___106.7%___

Price Graph: _____-_____ Balance of Power™: ___+____   **Note:**
Stochastics: _____-_____ Volume: _____+_____   *Never act upon less*
MoneyStream™: _-_____ Trend: _____+_____   *than a three plus (+++)*
Total score for this chart: _- - - +/++_____   *or a three minus (- - -)*
                                                    chart.

Evaluation: _____
  Cash Out: 5^5/_8$ = $5.625   X 1,000 = $5,625
  Cash In: 11^5/_8$ = $11.625   X 1,000 = $11,625
                                                    $6,000 Gain

  $6,000 / $5,625 = 106.7% Gain

Notice the MoneyStream™ is a negative, Balance of Power™ is good, the Price Graph is okay, and Stochastics are high. The chart did show an upward trend by the moving averages. Sometimes Stock Splits don't rely on what the indicators say. I purchased one April $90 Call on Lucent.

I evaluated this trade after I had closed out the position, and I did not follow the +++ rule. Don't buy anything other than a three plus. This was only a ++ chart. However, I would only have had to wait one day for my buy signal. Look at the chart for the next day.

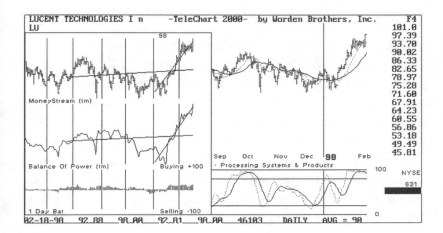

Now look. The Balance of Power™ has taken a nice upward movement, the MoneyStream™ has turned to a positive, and the Price Graph is now above both moving averages, in just one day!

Guess what, the rumor came out to be reliable. I closed out the position on the 19th (that is only two days later) for a profit of 106.67%. Yes, I doubled the money that I had invested in two days! Not bad for only a rumor.

Also, look at what happened over the next few weeks. Can you pick out all five entry strategies? Could you have played all five entry strategies?

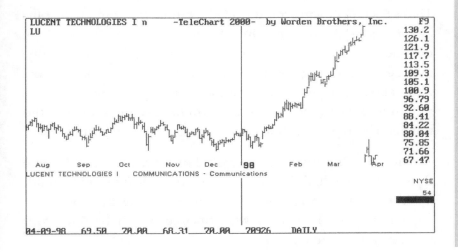

Notes:

Entry Point 2: The Announcement

The second entry point is when the actual announcement of a split occurs. When a stock split is announced during market hours, it is often possible to take advantage of the first few hours of upward movement. The stock almost always takes an immediate rise on the announcement of the split. On a big stock, the move will often last one to three days before the price settles back from profit taking. In Entry Point 2, immediate action is crucial. The instant the split is announced, you need to act. Sometimes within seconds or minutes, a rise in value will occur. Other investors are jumping in, which drives the price of the stock up.

Since timing is so crucial, if you want to consistently play this strategy, you need a reliable source of fast information. One such service is IQ Pager™. This is a service that pages you with up-to-the-minute, tradable information on an alphanumeric pager. Since you receive the information from such sources as Bloomberg, you may know about the split before your broker.

Let me show you an example of how this service, coupled with the strategy basics, works. One day in the fall of 1997, my pager went off with a page concerning a stock split announcement by Kansas City Southern Railroad, ticker symbol KCS.

I immediately called my broker and placed an order for three contracts of a call option at a premium of $5 per share. That's $500 per contract multiplied by three to equal $1,500 plus commissions. At the same time, I placed a GTC order to sell my contracts at $6 per share. All of this took place within one minute of receiving the page. I had taken immediate action. After about eight minutes from the time I got off the telephone with my broker, I received a call from him saying that he could not get my $6 price. I thought "Oh well, how much did I lose?"

He said, "By the time your GTC order reached the trading floor, the option had risen to 6^3/_4$ dollars." He thought I wouldn't mind the extra 75¢ profit. Remember all of this took only eight minutes. The "act now" principle will determine your success in this entry point.

One rule of thumb to remember for Stock Split Entry 2: *Never use a market order.*

I've heard many horror stories with the use of stock splits and market orders. You can act immediately but with the incorrect action. Let's say that, in the above example, you really wanted in. You get a page about the split announcement and you know it's going to be a good split. Since you know that the price of the stock is going to go up dramatically and you want to get in right away, you call your broker and tell him to purchase three contracts with a market order. This time, instead of your sell order not being filled at the price you determined, your buy order is in a very volatile position. As the price goes soaring up, your market order waits in line to be filled. The price is at $5, a market order is placed, and the order is filled at the high of the day of $8. Then your GTC of $6 is triggered during a volatile swing toward the end of the market. You just lost $600 ($8 minus $6 equals $2 times 100 shares per contract equals $200 multiplied by three contracts equals $600). Use a market order and you could potentially lose a good percentage of your money very quickly.

ENTRY POINT 3: POST SPLIT ANNOUNCEMENT

The next entry point is called the "post split announcement." Be sure to follow the charts to look at certain changes in the prices called DUCks (Dipping Undervalued Calls) to assist you in determining your entry level.

Basically, three to 10 days after the split announcement, the stock often shows a pattern of pulling back. Often, just after the stock rises on the announcement of the split, there will be some profit taking and the stock will drop back down temporarily. The Price Graph shows a downward trend. The moving averages may change direction. At this point there is a second opportunity to take advantage of the stock split announcement. You purchase on the dip. This strategy is good for those that cannot take advantage of entry point 2, the announcement.

Notes:

Watch the charts. You should visually confirm that the stock has pulled back or taken a little dip. Then wait a little bit more for the pattern to turn back to the upside. Your chart and especially the Price Graph should confirm the pattern and trend upward after the dip. Often there are three to four of these opportunities before the actual split date.

ENTRY POINT 4: PAY DATE SPLIT

The next entry point is called the pay date play. The time to enter at this point is two to three days before the actual split date. You then hold your options through the split and sell them one to three days after the split. This play historically has high odds of profit. If you want the odds to be in your favor, then consider this play. Practice it with Simutrades and see what you come up with because we are still dealing with a high risk, high volatility strategy.

Watch the stock pattern the week before the pay date. You should see a pattern of upward movement of the stock price, or in the worst case, the pattern should be sideways. If the pattern does not conform to the strategy and to your game plan, stay out and wait for another opportunity. It is not good to gamble with your money if you don't have to. The more factors that you have in your favor, the greater the odds that your play will become profitable.

What we are actually doing here is "riding the wave" or holding our option through the split. We may have one April $90 Call before the split, and two April $45 Calls after. Generally there exists a good upward movement directly after the split, and you may receive a sizable yield.

Download a stock split calendar to gather potential candidates. With a good stock split calendar you can view the splits for the entire month and it should indicate which splits have options available. Then, check out the charts and go through the Simutrade Worksheet. It seems to me that finding candidates for the Stock Split strategy is about as easy as it gets.

I've found a couple of calendars on the Internet at www.yahoo.com and www.stockinfo.standardpoor.com.

Yahoo/Briefing: Splits Calendar - Microsoft Internet Explorer   Page 2 of 3

Payable	Ex Date	Company	Symbol	Ratio	Announced	Optionable
Feb 02	Feb 03	First of Long Island	FLIC	3-2	Dec 17	-
	Feb 03	MTS Systems	MTSC	2-1	Dec 03	Yes
	Feb 03	Rite Aid Corp	RAD	2-1	Jan 07	Yes
	Feb 03	Superior Telecom	SUT	5-4	Jan 15	-
Feb 03	Feb 04	Applied Power	APW	2-1	Jan 09	-
Feb 04	Feb 05	Graco Inc	GGG	3-2	Dec 12	-
Feb 05	Feb 06	Albion Banc Corp	ALBC	3-2	Dec 22	-
	Feb 06	Pathfinder Bancorp	PBHC	3-2	Jan 15	-
Feb 06	Feb 09	Imperial Bancorp	IMP	3-2	Jan 21	Yes
	Feb 09	MacDermid	MACD	3-1	Jan 15	-
	Feb 09	Premier Bancshares	PMB	3-2	Jan 08	-
Feb 08	Feb 09	ASE Test Ltd	ASTSF	2-1	Jan 20	-
Feb 09	Feb 10	SLH Corp	SLHO	2-1	Jan 20	-
Feb 10	Feb 11	BFC Financial	BFCFA	3-1	Jan 15	-
	Feb 11	PennFed Fincl	PFSB	2-1	Jan 14	-
Feb 12	Feb 13	Antenna Products	ANTP	2-1	Jan 09	-
	Feb 13	Buckeye Partners	BPL	2-1	Jan 20	-

```
SPM 04/09 STOCK SPLITS    (Page 1 of 2)

     NAME (SYM)          AMOUNT    EX-DATE    REC-DATE   PAY-DATE   ANNOUNCED
State Auto Fin'l (STFC)  ** 2-for-1  --------  06/18/98   07/08/98   03/06/98
Farmers Capital (FFKT)   ** 2-for-1  --------  06/01/98   07/01/98   01/27/98
CNB Financial (CNBF)     ** 2-for-1  --------  06/15/98   06/30/98   02/27/98
Acacia Research (ACRI)   ** 2-for-1  --------  05/29/98   06/12/98   03/17/98
Intl Bancshares (IBOC)   ** 5-for-4  --------  05/22/98   06/12/98   03/23/98
Buckle Inc. (BKE)      R ** 3-for-2  06/09/98  05/28/98   06/08/98   03/25/98
GATX Corp. (GMT)         ** 2-for-1  --------  05/11/98   06/01/98   01/30/98
Household Intl. (HI)     ** 3-for-1  06/02/98  05/14/98   06/01/98   03/10/98
                SOURCE: S&P MARKETSCOPE
       STOCK SPLITS ALSO ON http://www.stockinfo.standardpoor.com

     NAME (SYM)          AMOUNT    EX-DATE    REC-DATE   PAY-DATE   ANNOUNCED
Abbott Laboratories (ABT)   2-for-1  06/01/98  05/01/98   05/29/98   02/13/98
Danaher Corp. (DHR)      ** 2-for-1  --------  --------   05/29/98   03/06/98
Fiserv Inc. (FISV)          3-for-2  06/01/98  05/15/98   05/29/98   03/24/98
LHS Group (LHSG)         ** 2-for-1  05/29/98  04/03/98   05/28/98   03/18/98
Belmont Bancorp (BLMT)   ** 2-for-1  --------  05/01/98   05/22/98   03/04/98
MSC Industrial Direct (MSM) 2-for-1  --------  04/24/98   05/22/98   04/06/98
Paychex Inc. (PAYX)         3-for-2  --------  05/08/98   05/22/98   04/09/98
Shorewood Packaging (SWD)   3-for-2  --------  05/02/98   05/22/98   04/01/98
                SOURCE: S&P MARKETSCOPE
```

One interesting way to maximize your profits on any Stock Split entry point while capping your loss would be to always purchase contracts in sets of two. If your options double in price, sell one. This means that you are even, plus you still have one option. Watch the charts and don't get too greedy. Put in a GTC order, or maybe a trailing stop loss order.

A trailing stop loss order would work something like this: Your option is at $8. You're put in a stop loss of $7. Your option

Notes:

increases to $9^1/_2$. Change your stop loss to $8^1/_2$, and so on. This way, if the option gets some bad news, other investors decide to take some profit, or whatever may make the price of your option go down, you have an order that can lock in profits and cap your loss.

ENTRY POINT 5: POST STOCK SPLIT

The next entry point is called the "post split date." This requires watching for the long term DUCks on the charts. Trading basics like charts and fundamental analysis will help determine what options you purchase. This is a longer-term play (usually) and requires more time for review. You should log at least 10 Simutrades prior to an actual cash trade on all of the Stock Split plays, especially this one.

If you look at the historical chart (in the beginning of this chapter), you will notice that often the price of a stock will split and then gradually rise back to the previous high price before the split. The stock tends to regain the ground it gave up on the split and often attains its former price range. This rise could take a few months to a few years. If the basics of the company and the other conditions that drove the stock to split in the first place don't change, it will almost always move back up to its former range. Some stocks even have "split ranges." Whenever the price of the stock reaches a certain range, the stock historically has split.

If you like Entry Point 5, then consider watching and trading this same stock like it was a Rolling Option. It should really be called a Range Rider Option because of the upward movement in trend (draw some trendlines and show support and resistance). Whatever you call it, there will most probably be dips and peaks along the way. You can take advantage of this and roll the options. Make sure and fill out a new Simutrade Worksheet for each trade. Don't just assume that something has not changed. Check the chart. Check the P/E. Watch the trend and breakouts through the trendlines.

You can use any of these five entry point strategies. I find that usually people pick one, maybe two strategies that best fit their Time Temperament. If you don't have a pager or news service, consider playing Entry Points 3 to 5, and use a Stock Split Calendar.

In the Stock Split examples in this chapter, I did not use GTC orders. Instead, I decided to watch my open positions more closely and get out at my pre-determined exit points. My game plan targeted a profit of between 25 and 100%. I also purchased options farther out. This gave me more time and security.

STOCK SPLITS EXAMPLE 2

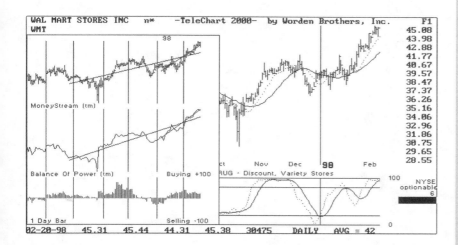

EVALUATION

Wal-Mart announced a split on 2/20. I checked the chart and decided to purchase 10 June $40 Calls at 6^{1}/_{2}$. On March 2, I decided to sell at 7^{7}/_{8}$. This play was taking a little longer than I had anticipated and I did not want to wait any longer. My profit was a little under my target of 25%, but I still consider this a successful trade.

Notes:

Notes:

SIMUTRADE STOCK SPLITS WORKSHEET

Strategy: ____Announcement_____
                    (Preannouncement, Announcement, Post Announcement, DUCk, et cetera)

Date: _02/20/98_ Time: ___1:00____   Broker: Simutrade_____

Company: _Wal Mart Stores, Inc.____ Ticker: _WMT____ Quote: _____ X $45^5/$_8$__

Split Date: _____ Split Ratio: _____

Option: _Jun $40 Call___ Option Ticker: __WMTFH_____ Quote: _____ X $6^1/$_2$__

Notes: __Watch every day for exits._____

_____

Contracts Purchased: ___10_____   Price: __$6^1/$_2$_____

Exit Strategy: ___Target: 25 - 100%_____

Associated GTCs placed: _____

Closing Trade: __10 @ $7^7/$_8$____ Date: __03/02/98__ Net Gain/Loss: ___21.15%___

Price Graph: _____o_____	Balance of Power™: ___+____	**Note:**
Stochastics: _____o_____	Volume: _____+___	*Never act upon less*
MoneyStream™: _+_____	Trend: _____+___	*than a three plus (+++)*
Total score for this chart: _oo++/++_		*or a three minus (- - -)* *chart.*

Evaluation: _____
   Cash Out: $6^1/$_2$ = $6.50   X 1,000 = $6,500_____
   Cash In: $7^7/$_8$ = $7.875   X 1,000 = $7,875_____
   _____ $1,375 Gain_____

   _$1,375 / $6,500 = 21.15% Gain_____

   _____
   _____
   _____
   _____
   _____
   _____
   _____

STOCK SPLITS EXAMPLE 3

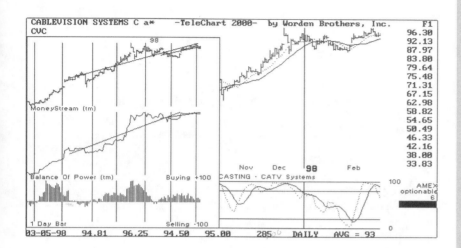

EVALUATION

CVC announced a stock split on 3/5. Here, the chart showed a mixed buy signal at best. It seems that when a company announces a stock split, the chart may or may not give you a buy signal. I don't know of any indicators that are always accurate with Stock Splits.

I decided to buy 10 June $90 Calls at $12. This gave me a Cash Out of $12,000. I watched the charts and got a quote every day. When the price of the option reached $20, I decided to sell. I made over $8,000 on this trade in nine days. Could I have made more? Yes. Take a look at the chart on page 125.

Notes:

SIMUTRADE STOCK SPLITS WORKSHEET

Strategy: ___Announcement_____
(Preannouncement, Announcement, Post Announcement, DUCk, et cetera)

Date: __03/05/98__ Time: ___1:00_____ Broker: __Simutrade_____

Company: _Cable Vision Systems___ Ticker: _CVC____ Quote: _____ X _$95___

Split Date: _____ Split Ratio: _____

Option: _Jun $90 Call___ Option Ticker: __CVCFR_____ Quote: _____ X _$12___

Notes: __Watch every day for exits._____

_____

Contracts Purchased: ___10_____ Price: __$12_____

Exit Strategy: ____Target: 25 - 100%_____

Associated GTCs placed: _____

_____

Closing Trade: _10 @ 20^7/_8_ Date: __03/16/98__ Net Gain/Loss: ___74%_____

Price Graph: ___o____ Balance of Power™: ___o____		*Note:*
Stochastics: ____-____ Volume: _____ +		*Never act upon less*
MoneyStream™: _+____ Trend: _____ +		*than a three plus (+++)*
Total score for this chart: _o - ++/o+_		*or a three minus (- - -)* *chart.*

Evaluation: _____
  Cash Out: $12   = $12.00   X 1,000 = $12,000
  Cash In: 20^7/_8$ = $20.875   X 1,000 = $20,875
                                                      $8,875 Gain

  _$8,875 / $12,000 = 74% Gain_____

_____
_____
_____
_____
_____
_____
_____
_____

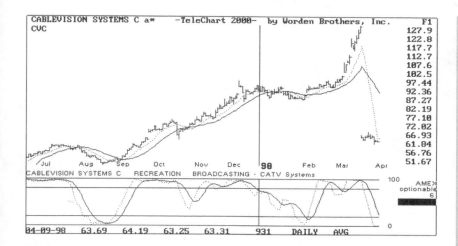

The price of the stock was at $95 when I purchased my options. You can see by the chart that the price of the stock rose to over $127 before the split. That's over 30 points of movement in about a month. The price of the option would have increased at least that amount. Why did I get out? Because I was happy with my results and I did not want to get greedy. I was well within my game plan.

Notes:

STOCK SPLITS EXAMPLE 4

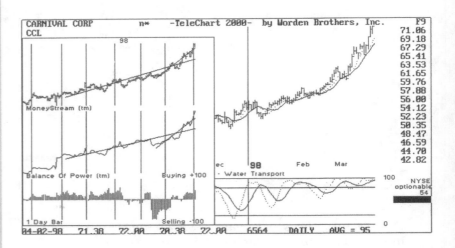

EVALUATION

I was reading W.I.N.™ on 4/2 and Wade mentioned that Carnival was going to have a Board of Directors meeting soon and that this could be a Stock Split candidate. I decided to purchase on the rumor and Simutraded one July $70 Call at $6³/₈. I watched the chart and got a quote every day. On 4/7/98 I decided to get out at $8³/₄ when the price started taking a downward trend. You could say that I "lost" $4 on this trade as the options were trading around $12 on the 6th, two days before. I say that it doesn't matter since I made 37.3%. This is a nice profit and well within my game plan.

SIMUTRADE STOCK SPLITS WORKSHEET

Strategy: ___Preannouncement___
(Preannouncement, Announcement, Post Announcement, DUCk, et cetera)

Date: _04/02/98_ Time: __1:00__ Broker: _Simutrade_

Company: _Carnival Corporation_ Ticker: _CCL_ Quote: _____ X $69^3/$_4$

Split Date: _____ Split Ratio: _____

Option: _Jul $70 Call_ Option Ticker: _CCLGN_ Quote: _____ X $6^3/$_8$

Notes: _Watch every day for exits._
_____

Contracts Purchased: __10_____ Price: _$6^3/$_8$___

Exit Strategy: ___Target: 25 - 100%___

Associated GTCs placed: _____

Closing Trade: _10 @ $8^3/$_4_ Date: _04/17/98_ Net Gain/Loss: _37.3%_

Price Graph: ___-___ Balance of Power™: __+__	Stochastics: ___-___ Volume: ___+___	MoneyStream™: _+_ Trend: ___+___	Total score for this chart: _- - ++/++_

Note:
Never act upon less than a three plus (+++) or a three minus (- - -) chart.

Evaluation: _____

Cash Out:	$6^3/$_8$	=	$6.375	X 1,000 =	$6,375
Cash In:	$8^3/$_4$	=	$8.75	X 1,000 =	$8,750
					$2,375 Gain

$2,375 / $6,375 = 37.3% Gain

STOCK SPLITS EXAMPLE 5

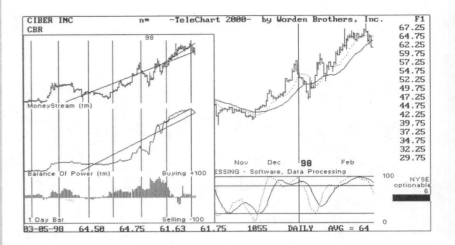

EVALUATION

After I evaluated this trade, I realized I should have never gotten in. It was only a + chart, although the Volume and Trend were positive. This means that I probably needed to have more details in the entrance portion of my game plan.

Even though I broke a rule, Stock Splits excited me. I wanted to play every one. On CBR I purchased one August $65 Call for $7⅞ on the day of the stock split announcement, 3/5/98. I watched the charts (it only took a short while for the chart to go up to +++, so I

SIMUTRADE STOCK SPLITS WORKSHEET

Strategy: ___Announcement___
(Preannouncement, Announcement, Post Announcement, DUCk, et cetera)

Date: _03/05/98_ Time: ___1:00___   Broker: _Simutrade_

Company: _Ciber, Inc._   Ticker: _CBR_   Quote: _____ X $36^3/$_8$

Split Date: _____   Split Ratio: _____

Option: _Aug $65 Call_   Option Ticker: _CBRHM_   Quote: _____ X $7^7/$_8$

Notes: _Watch every day for exits._

Contracts Purchased: ___1___   Price: _$7^7/$_8$_

Exit Strategy: ___Target: 25 - 100%___

Associated GTCs placed: _____

Closing Trade: _1 @ $11^1/$_8$_   Date: _03/27/98_   Net Gain/Loss: _41.3%_

		Note:
Price Graph: __+__	Balance of Power™: __-__	
Stochastics: __-__	Volume: __+__	Never act upon less than a three plus (+++) or a three minus (- - -) chart.
MoneyStream™: __-__	Trend: __+__	
Total score for this chart: _+ - - - /++_		

Evaluation: _____

Cash Out:	$7^7/$_8$	=	$7.875	X 100 =	$787.50
Cash In:	$11^1/$_8$	=	$11.125	X 100 =	$1,112.50
					$325.00 Gain

$325 / $787.50 = 41.3% Gain

would not have had to wait long). Then I sold on 3/27 for $11^1/$_8$. This was a 41.3% profit of $1,112.50.

In hindsight, I should have waited the extra days to enter the trade, or made a decision to play one of the other entry points. The chart is a good footprint of a Stock Split. Look at the chart for 4/9, after the split.

Notes:

STOCK SPLITS EXAMPLE 6

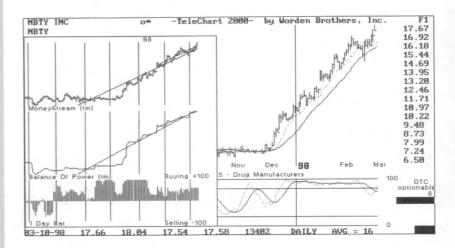

EVALUATION

This has to be one of my favorite trades—and also one of the reasons that greed creeps in. If you look on the Simutrade Worksheet, you can see that I made 126% profit in less than a month. I more than doubled my money! Does this happen all the time? Definitely not. But it does happen often enough to make some very good cash flow.

My next step in fine-tuning my Stock Split game plan will be to try and find a way to make returns like this more consistently. Is it risky? Yes. Are the returns worth it? Probably.

Anyway, here is one of my favorite Simutrades. I purchased 10 contracts of NBTY June $50 Calls at $9 on the announcement day of 3/10 after looking at the chart. I waited and checked the chart every day. It climbed, and climbed and climbed. At 100% I said, "Wow" and started getting nervous. I bought in when the stock was around $17. Look at the chart of 4/9 on page 132.

SIMUTRADE STOCK SPLITS WORKSHEET

Strategy: ___Announcement___
(Preannouncement, Announcement, Post Announcement, DUCk, et cetera)

Date: _03/10/98_ Time: ___1:00___ Broker: Simutrade

Company: _NBTY, Inc._ Ticker: __NBTY__ Quote: _____ X $17^5/$_8$

Split Date: _____ Split Ratio: _____

Option: _Jun $50 Call_ Option Ticker: __NBQFJ__ Quote: _____ X $9

Notes: __Watch every day for exits.__

Contracts Purchased: ___10___ Price: _$9_

Exit Strategy: ___Target: 25 - 100%___

Associated GTCs placed: _____

Closing Trade: _10 @ $20^3/$_8$_ Date: __04/03/98__ Net Gain/Loss: ___126.4%___

Price Graph: ____-____ Balance of Power™: ___+___

Stochastics: ____o____ Volume: _____+____

MoneyStream™: __+__ Trend: _____+____

Total score for this chart: _-o++/++_

Note:
Never act upon less than a three plus (+++) or a three minus (- - -) chart.

Evaluation: _____

Cash Out:	$9	= $9.00	X 1,000 =	$9,000
Cash In:	$20^3/$_8$	= $20.375	X 1,000 =	$20,375
				$11,375 Gain

$11,375 / $9,000 = 126.4% Gain

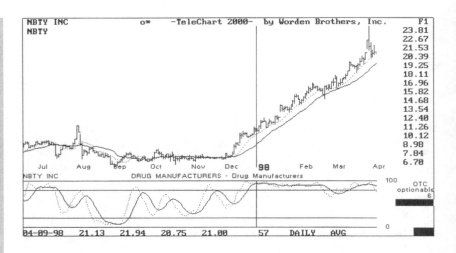

I guess you could say that I "chickened out" and sold right after I got to 100%. I sold partly because this was on my game plan and partly because I was elated with my return and could not stand losing one penny. I liked what I had. I was happy. Why take more? Could I have made more? Maybe.

Maybe I would have been better off concentrating on executing each entry point more exactly to maximize my profit potential on each split. I really don't care. I just made 126% on one trade and I don't have a care in the world.

STOCK SPLITS EXAMPLE 7

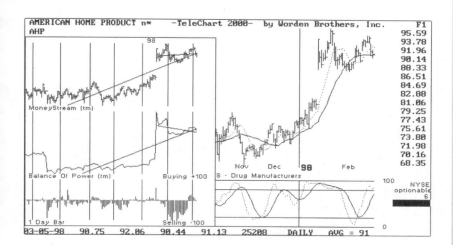

EVALUATION

Here is another example of Entry Point 2. I found that I tended to like this strategy. I have access to news about stock splits and I like the easy strategy basics. Also, check out the gap in January. Could this be some rumors or insider trading price gap about the split? I don't know, maybe it's just some good news. I plan on putting AHP on my stock split watch list and check it again when the price reaches the $70+ range, at the same time next year.

On the announcement of a stock split on 3/5, I purchased one July $90 Call at $8 1/4. I watched the indicators on the chart and got a quote each day (usually after the closing in the evenings because this is when I have the time). I sold my option on 3/11 at $11 5/8 for a profit of $337.50 or 40.9%.

Notes:

SIMUTRADE STOCK SPLITS WORKSHEET

Strategy: ___Announcement___
(Preannouncement, Announcement, Post Announcement, DUCk, et cetera)

Date: _03/05/98_ Time: __1:00__ Broker: _Simutrade_

Company: _American Home Products_ Ticker: _AHP_ Quote: _____ X 91^1/_8$

Split Date: _____ Split Ratio: _____

Option: _Jun $90 Call_ Option Ticker: _AHPGR_ Quote: _____ X 8^1/_4$

Notes: _Watch every day for exits._

Contracts Purchased: ___1___ Price: _8^1/_4$

Exit Strategy: ___Target: 25 - 100%___

Associated GTCs placed: _____

Closing Trade: _1 @ 11^5/_8_ Date: _03/11/98_ Net Gain/Loss: _40.9%_

		Note:
Price Graph: ___+___ Balance of Power™: __+__		*Never act upon less*
Stochastics: ___-___ Volume: _____+		*than a three plus (+++)*
MoneyStream™: _-_ Trend: _____+		*or a three minus (- - -)*
Total score for this chart: _+ - - +/++_		*chart.*

Evaluation: _____
Cash Out:	8^1/_4$	=	$8.25	X 100 =	$825.00
Cash In:	11^5/_8$	=	$11.625	X 100 =	$1,162.50
					$337.50 Gain

$337.50 / $825.00 = 40.9% Gain

STOCK SPLITS EXAMPLE 8

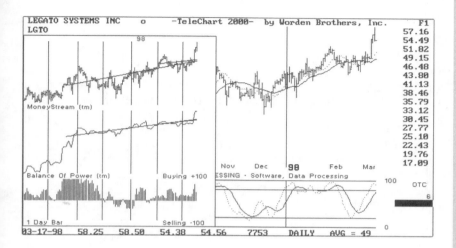

EVALUATION

I purchased call options on Legato Systems when they announced the split on 3/17. Again I watched the charts and the prices of the options. I remember distinctly that this trade bothered me. It seemed to take too long. It helped me narrow down my Time Temperament. I've had longer trades, some a lot longer than 20 days.

Maybe I should try out intra-day trading. My only drawback right now is the lack of a good source of up-to-the-minute prices, and the time to pay attention to them if I did have a source.

With Stock Splits you can be in and out in a very short period of time. In this trade I was out in 20 days (even if it did bother me) with a profit of $412.50 or 68.7%.

Notes:

SIMUTRADE STOCK SPLITS WORKSHEET

Strategy: _____ Announcement _____
(Preannouncement, Announcement, Post Announcement, DUCk, et cetera)

Date: _03/17/98_ Time: ___1:00_____ Broker: _Simutrade_____

Company: _Legato Systems_____ Ticker: _LGTO___ Quote: _____ X 54^9/_{16}$_

Split Date: _____ Split Ratio: _____

Option: _Jun $55 Call___ Option Ticker: __EQNFK_____ Quote: _____ X _$6_____

Notes: __Watch every day for exits._____

_____

Contracts Purchased: ___10_____ Price: __$6_____

Exit Strategy: _____Target: 25 - 100%_____

Associated GTCs placed: _____

_____

Closing Trade: _10 @ 10^1/_8$___ Date: _04/07/98_ Net Gain/Loss: ___68.7%___

Price Graph: ____-___	Balance of Power™: ___+_____	**Note:**
Stochastics: ____-___	Volume: _____ +	*Never act upon less*
MoneyStream™: _+___	Trend: _____ +	*than a three plus (+++)*
Total score for this chart: _- - ++/++_		*or a three minus (- - -)* *chart.*

Evaluation: _____

Cash Out:	$6	=	$6.00	X 1,000 =	$6,000
Cash In:	10^1/_8$	=	$10.125	X 1,000 =	$10,125
					$4,125 Gain

_$4,125 / $6,000 = 68.7% Gain_____

_____
_____
_____
_____
_____
_____
_____
_____

Notes:

Stock Transaction Tracking Record

| | OPEN | | | | | | | | | CLOSE | | | | | |
Date	Stock	Price	B/S	Qty	Position	O/C	Ord	Fill $	Total	Date	B/S	Qty	Fill $	Total	Comms
2/17	LU	86⁹/₃₂	B	10	Apr 90 C		1	5⁵/₈	5,625	2/19	S	10	11⁵/₈	11,625	
Strategy	Stock Split									P/L $	6,000	Days	2	Yield	106.7 %
2/20	WMT	45³/₈	B	10	Jun 40 C		2	6¹/₂	6,500	3/2	S	10	7⁷/₈	7,875	
Strategy	Stock Split #2									P/L $	1,375	Days	10	Yield	21.1 %
3/5	CVC	95	B	10	Jun 90 C		3	12	12,000	3/16	S	10	20⁷/₈	20,875	
Strategy	Stock Split #2									P/L $	8,875	Days	11	Yield	74 %
4/2	CCL	69³/₄	B	10	Jul 70 C		4	6⁷/₈	6,375	4/17	S	10	8³/₄	8,750	
Strategy	Stock Split #1									P/L $	2,375	Days	15	Yield	37.3 %
3/5	CBR	36³/₈	B	1	Aug 65 C		5	7⁷/₈	787.50	3/27	S	1	11¹/₈	1,112.50	
Strategy	Stock Split									P/L $	325	Days	22	Yield	41.3 %
3/10	NBTY	17⁵/₈	B	10	Jun 50 C		6	9	9,000	4/3	S	10	20³/₈	20,375	
Strategy	Stock Split									P/L $	11,375	Days	24	Yield	126.4 %
3/5	AHP	91¹/₈	B	1	Jul 90 C		7	8¹/₄	825	3/11	S	1	11⁵/₈	1,162.50	
Strategy	Stock Split									P/L $	337.50	Days	6	Yield	40.9 %
3/17	LGTO	54⁹/₁₆	B	10	Jun 55 C		8	6	6,000	4/7	S	10	10¹/₈	10,125	
Strategy	Stock Split									P/L $	4,125	Days	20	Yield	68.7 %
Strategy	Notes									P/L $		Days		Yield	%

CHAPTER 12
Peaks And Slams

Peaks and Slams are two strategies that use news as a benchmark for information entry points. The announcement of earnings either positive or negative will have a tendency to make the stock price jump from 5 to 25% in a short period of time. The change in the stock price could either be in a positive direction or a negative direction depending upon the news. Mergers and acquisitions have quite an effect on stock prices. Changes in top management can also bring about dramatic changes in the pricing of a stock. Buy back offers tend to drive stock prices in either direction.

The IQ Pager™ announces many dramatic stock price changes throughout the day. Time is of utmost importance if one is going to be successful at this strategy. You must react quickly to maximize your profit potential. The strategies are very simple to understand.

THE STEPS

To play Peaks or Slams, you must first select candidates and gather information. The Wealth Information Network™ (W.I.N.™) is an excellent resource to use. The IQ Pager™ is probably one of the best sources of almost instant information concerning changes. Each day, *The Wall Street Journal* publishes a section called the "Price Percentage Gainers and Losers." This

Notes:

Notes:

section lists stocks that moved dramatically either up (Percentage Gainers) or down (Percentage Losers). It also shows the volume of trades that were done. This statistic is an important parameter, as you will want to purchase a stock that has a volume above 200,000.

You can also use TeleChart 2000© to find Peaks and Slams. TeleChart© has filtered out three areas in their system to identify these percentage gappers. The search engine filters are titled gappers, volume search, and the 52-week highs and lows. I suggest you evaluate each of these resources to enhance your knowledge and to find a source that works for you. You may want to make a different Simutrade account for each news source. Then compare which one works best by the quality and quantity of successful trades.

Look at the charts, check with your broker, and review the fundamentals to validate the information that you have gathered. Determine if the information you have received is transient or volatile enough to play. Remember that you must establish your exit point before you enter the trade. Update your news research to make sure your information is current. Remember this point: Good news is short lived, while bad news can linger for quite some time.

Use the Simutrade System to perfect and master the skills necessary to use the Peaks and Slams strategies effectively. Do as many Simutrades as necessary for you to feel comfortable trading Peaks and Slams.

PEAKS

The Peak strategy is used when a stock's price has dramatically risen in a short time frame. Usually this change is in response to news of impending changes in the company. A takeover by a larger company sometimes drives the stock price up dramatically. Many times rumors of these takeovers will affect stock prices. There could be many reasons that the Peak has occurred.

Once you have found a stock that fits into your parameter for purchase in your game plan, buy a put with the nearest lower strike price and the month closest to the current date. Use a limit order (and order for a specific price) and not a market order (an order for whatever the current price is) as the price of the stock could be at an artificial high. Check your charts. Make sure you have a triple minus,---, (remember, we are purchasing a put and we want the price of the stock to go back down). Once your order is filled, proceed to place a GTC sell order to close your position once your stock has arrived at your exit point.

SLAMS

As you browse the charts, look for a stock whose price has just recently been slammed, or the price of the stock has gone down from 5 to 25% of its value. The time frame could be from a few minutes to a few days. Once you have found a stock that meets your parameters, buy the nearest lower strike price and the closest month. Use limit orders when buying these calls.

Sometimes news will drive a stock so that its price is artificially inflated. Be careful, and make sure that you check the news. When your order is filled, place a GTC sell order to close your position when the stock price arrives at your exit point.

Always remember: *Don't get greedy!* You are targeting a small chunk of profit in a short period of time. It doesn't take much to create good growth for your account. I have had several trades that have been initially positive only to turn sour because I waited too long looking for just a little more upward movement in the stock price. I got greedy and I paid the price.

Let's look at some good Peaks and Slams candidate stocks. We will try to evaluate some of the news that made the stocks candidates for these strategies.

PEAKS AND SLAMS EXAMPLE 1

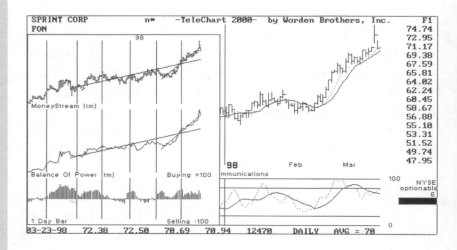

EVALUATION

Here we find a Peak; the stock price appears to be at a very high point, it appears the chart has it at a 52-week high. I decided to jump in right away after a look at the chart.

I bought ten April $70 Puts for $2¹/₄. I calculate my target profit of 25% to be $2¹³/₁₆, so I place a GTC order to sell at $2¹³/₁₆. I also calculate my Stop Loss at $1¹³/₁₆, targeting a 20% loss.

On 2/27 my GTC order is filled for a profit of $562.50 or 25%. This fits my game plan just fine.

SIMUTRADE PEAKS AND SLAMS WORKSHEET

Date: 03/23/98   Time: 1:00   Broker: Simutrade
Company: Sprint Corp   Ticker: FON   Quote: _____ X $70^{13}/₁₆
P/E: _____   News: _____
Notes: _____

Option: Apr $70 Call   Option Ticker: _____   Quote: _____ X $2^{1}/₄
Contracts Purchased: 10   Price: $2^{1}/₄
Exit Strategy: Target 25%. $2^{1}/₄ x 1.25 = $2.8125 = $2^{13}/₁₆
Associated GTCs placed: Sell 10 @ $2^{13}/₁₆

Closing Trade: 10 @ $2^{13}/₁₆   Date: 03/27/98   Net Gain/Loss: 25%

Price Graph: ___-___ Balance of Power™: ___+___   *Note:*
Stochastics: __-/o__ Volume: ___+___   *Never act upon less*
MoneyStream™: __-__ Trend: ___+___   *than a three plus (+++)*
Total score for this chart: __- o - +/++__   *or a three minus (- - -)*
                                                    chart.

Evaluation: _____
  Cash Out: $2^{1}/₄   = $2.25   X 1,000 = $2,250.00
  Cash In: $2^{13}/₁₆ = $2.8125 X 1,000 = $2,812.50
                                                    $562.50 Gain

  $562.50 / $2,250 = 25% Gain

Notes:

PEAKS AND SLAMS EXAMPLE 2

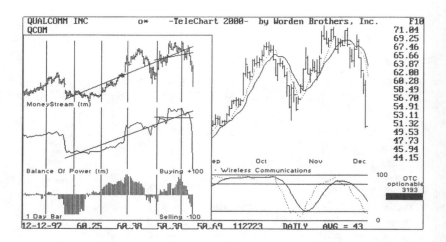

EVALUATION

This looked like a good slam going into the trade. The chart looks okay and the Price Graph shows that the stock is really at a bargain. But, the stock continued down. I missed my target loss by a little, but I got out with only a 29.2% loss. That's kind of high, but it's okay.

If the trade is not doing what you want it to do, get out. Put your money to some better use. Don't worry about losing money every now and then.

SIMUTRADE PEAKS AND SLAMS WORKSHEET

Date: 12/12/97   Time: 1:00   Broker: Simutrade

Company: Qualcomm, Inc.   Ticker: QCOM   Quote: _____ X 50^{11}/_{16}$

P/E: _____   News: _____

Notes: _____

Option: Jan $50 Call   Option Ticker: _____   Quote: _____ X $6

Contracts Purchased: 10   Price: $6

Exit Strategy: Target 25%. $6 x 1.25 = 7^{1}/_{2}$

Associated GTCs placed: Sell 10 @ 7^{1}/_{2}$

Closing Trade: 10 @ 4^{1}/_{4}$ Date: 12/19/97   Net Gain/Loss: <29.2%>

Price Graph: +	Balance of Power™: o	**Note:**
Stochastics: -	Volume: +	*Never act upon less*
MoneyStream™: o	Trend: o	*than a three plus (+++)*
Total score for this chart: + - oo/+o		*or a three minus (- - -)*
		chart.

Evaluation: _____

Cash Out:	$6	=	$6.00	X 1,000 =	$6,000
Cash In:	4^{1}/_{4}$	=	$4.25	X 1,000 =	$4,250
					$1,750 Loss

$1,750 / $6,000 = 29.2% Loss

Notes:

PEAKS AND SLAMS EXAMPLE 3

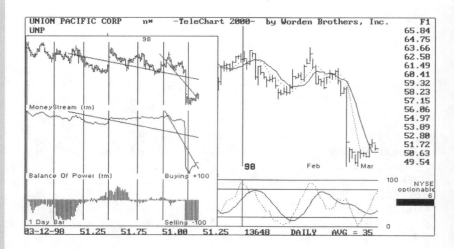

EVALUATION

Here is an interesting twist. I found the Slam, looked at the chart, and decided to purchase 10 contracts of the March $50 Calls. When I looked at the price of the options I thought that the stock had potential to increase as to get a really good return on my options. So, I put in two GTCs: one to sell 5 at $1⅞ and one to sell 5 at $2⅞.

Oh, the wonder of the GTC. I was filled on both orders on the same day. When you average out the returns, I ended up with a 58.3% return. Why did I do it this way? Why not?

SIMUTRADE PEAKS AND SLAMS WORKSHEET

Date: 03/12/98 Time: 1:00   Broker: Simutrade

Company: Union Pacific Corp   Ticker: UNP   Quote: _____ X 51^1/_4$

P/E: _____   News: _____

Notes: _____
_____

Option: Mar $50 Call   Option Ticker: _____   Quote: _____ X 1^1/_2$

Contracts Purchased: 10   Price: 1^1/_2$

Exit Strategy: Target 25%. 1^1/_2$ x 1.25 = 1^7/_8$

Associated GTCs placed: Sell 5 @ 1^7/_8$, Sell 5 @ 2^7/_8$
_____

Closing Trade: 5@ 1$^7/_8$, 5@ 2$^7/_8$ Date: 03/16/98   Net Gain/Loss: _____ 58.3%

Price Graph: _____+_____ Balance of Power™: _____-_____

Stochastics: _____o_____ Volume: _____ +

MoneyStream™: __+__ Trend: _____ +

Total score for this chart: __+o+ - /++__

Note:
Never act upon less than a three plus (+++) or a three minus (- - -) chart.

Evaluation: _____

Cash Out:	1^1/_2$	= $1.50	X 1,000 =	$1,500.00
Cash In:	1^7/_8$	= $1.875	X 500 =	$937.50
Cash In:	2^7/_8$	= $2.875	X 500 =	$1,437.50
				$875 Gain

$875 / $1,500 = 58.3% Gain

Notes:

PEAKS AND SLAMS EXAMPLE 4

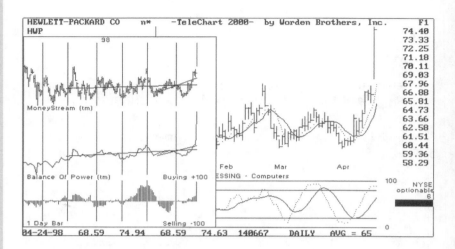

EVALUATION

This is another twist on this strategy—another way to play. Instead of getting into the trade after the big jump in price, why not profit from the jump. The only way that I know how to do this is to have an accurate, prompt news service.

I received news about HWP early in the morning. I looked at the opening price and noticed that there was a gap. I got a quote and looked at the chart. It was still early in the day so I decided to go for it.

I purchased 10 May $65 Calls at $3¹/₈ and placed a GTC order at $4, which is a little over my 25% target. I was filled the same day for a one-day profit of $875 or 28%. Don't you wish you could do that every day?

SIMUTRADE PEAKS AND SLAMS WORKSHEET

Date: 04/24/98   Time: 1:00   Broker: Simutrade

Company: Hewlett Packard   Ticker: HWP   Quote: _____ X $74^5/$_8$

P/E: _____   News: _____

Notes: _____

Option: May $65 Call   Option Ticker: _____   Quote: _____ X $3^1/$_8$

Contracts Purchased: 10   Price: $3^1/$_8$

Exit Strategy: Target 25%. $3^1/$_8$ x 1.25 = $3.90

Associated GTCs placed: Sell 10 @ $4

Closing Trade: 10 @ $4   Date: 04/24/97   Net Gain/Loss: 28%

		Note:
Price Graph: _____ -	Balance of Power™: ____ +	**Never act upon less**
Stochastics: ____ o	Volume: ____ +	*than a three plus (+++)*
MoneyStream™: __ +	Trend: ____ +	*or a three minus (- - -)*
Total score for this chart: _ - o ++/++		*chart.*

Evaluation: _____

Cash Out:	$3^1/$_8$	= $3.125	X 1,000 =	$3,125
Cash In:	$4	= $4.00	X 1,000 =	$4,000
				$875 Gain

$875 / $3,125 = 28% Gain

Notes:

STOCK TRANSACTION TRACKING RECORD

OPEN										CLOSE					
Date	Stock	Price	B/S	Qty	Position	O/C	Ord	Fill $	Total	Date	B/S	Qty	Fill $	Total	Comms
3/23	FON	70¹⁵/₁₆	B	10	Apr 70 P		1	2¹/₄	2,250	3/27	S	10	2¹⁵/₁₆	2,812.50	
Strategy	Peaks & Slams			Notes						P/L $	562.50		Days 4	Yield	25 %
12/12	QCOM	50¹¹/₁₆	B	10	Jan 50 C		2	6	6,000	12/19	S	10	4¹/₄	4,250	
Strategy	Peaks & Slams			Notes						P/L $	1,750		Days	Yield	-29.2 %
3/12	UNP	15¹/₄	B	10	Mar 50 C		3	1¹/₂	1,500	3/16	S	5	1⁷/₈	937.50	
Strategy	Peaks & Slams			Notes						P/L $			Days	Yield	%
							3a			3/16	S	5	2⁷/₈	1,437.50	
Strategy				Notes						P/L $	937.50		Days 4	Yield	58.3 %
4/24	HWP	74⁵/₈	B	10	May 65 C		4	3¹/₈	3,150	4/24	S	10	4	4,000	
Strategy	Peaks & Slams			Notes						P/L $	875		Days 1	Yield	28 %
Strategy				Notes						P/L $			Days	Yield	%
Strategy				Notes						P/L $			Days	Yield	%
Strategy				Notes						P/L $			Days	Yield	%
Strategy				Notes						P/L $			Days	Yield	%

CHAPTER 13
Options On News

The basics of Options on News are quite simple: Find some news and buy a call or a put, depending upon the news. If you have good news, generally you buy a call. If you have bad news, generally you buy a put. You get in, grab a quick little piece of profit, and get out. Use GTC orders, and resist the urge to be greedy. Little jumps in price can produce a good short-term yield. Doing this little jump can, many times, produce a number of small profits.

This strategy could work well for people who have a short Time Temperament, since the effect of news on the price of a stock is usually short lived. You will often find that your plays on news are over in a matter of days, often in merely hours.

This is an excellent strategy to practice Simutrades. You can get feedback in days, instead of weeks or months. Some strategies, like Rolling Stocks, can take weeks or months to play out before you know your closing trade and thus your yield. You must wait a "relatively" long-time. When you employ the Options on News strategy, the time frame is relatively short. A relatively lengthy long-term strategy might be to build the blue chip portion of your portfolio—stocks that you may want to hold on to for years.

Notes:

Notes:

How you define long-term depends upon your Time Temperament. Even if you never do any actual cash trades using Options on News, I would suggest that you Simutrade.

Playing the Options on News strategy has a somewhat elusive use. When you purchase a call, and then the stock drops out, the most probable answer will be found in the news. If you play the news strategy, it can teach you to be familiar with the cause and effect that different kinds of news have. Do you think learning about news can strengthen your other strategies? Yes.

If a stock price misses your target, and goes against your game plan, the most probable reason is news. If you have access to a good news service, you may be able to access information about your holdings and close trades in a timely manner to cap your losses. Yes, you can use news to cap your losses and still produce little chunks of profit.

Can you play bad news? Certainly. Practice buying puts. Use bad news, or negative news, to your advantage. Use the news as an indicator of a possible buy. Still check the charts. Remember, when buying puts you want to have a --- chart or better for a green light signal. If you are playing good news, change your target to a +++ chart. In either case, make sure you find the P/E and check it against your game plan.

The new TeleChart 2000© Version 4.0 for Windows 95/NT can scan for P/E ratios that you target. Just rev up your charting service of choice when you find candidates on news.

Personally, I concentrate my attention on things going up, and therefore usually discard bad news. Optimism is more appealing to me. I like things to increase since that is what my game plan says. If I concentrate on increase as a part of the strategy that I select, it can be easier to focus my attention on the increase of my portfolio.

It can be exciting to win with the market going up. That's news too. What is the overall market doing? Where do you find what is going on in the market? Is it up, down, or unchanged?

Is some big news story happening with a good solid company that I can invest in and employ the Options on News strategy? Is there some earth-shattering news that may affect the whole market including your open positions?

To answer this and other questions about news, you need to have a good source of news, or you must be diligent and have time to expend. A pager is a great way to get news about the goings on in the market. Find a paging service that produces the type of news that you are after.

If you use a pager, it is best to also find another source of news, usually on the Internet, or in print. I would not recommend using printed news if you want optimum trade results. In today's day and age we have electronic advantages like the Internet, web browsing, on line buying, e-mail reminders alerting you of news, and many other things. You should consult the printed news so that you know the whole story. Usually a pager or news wire service is very limited in their description of a news event. They have a limited amount of characters. You get the exact information that you need and no more. Make sure you know what is going on with your piece of news. Examples in this book are from the IQ Pager™ service.

TYPES OF NEWS

1. ACQUISITIONS AND TAKEOVERS

This is the news that one company is buying out or purchasing another company. The buyout is usually done by purchasing enough stock to own a majority of the shares outstanding and, therefore, have control and literally own the company.

Often, there is a bid offer. The purchasing company offers a bid to buy so many shares of stock at a particular price, usually a few percentage points over the current value.

It is usually best to purchase call options on the company being taken over. Companies that have been taken over very frequently go up.

Notes:

Notes:

2. SPIN-OFFS

When a new company is formed from a "parent" company, the new company is called a "spin-off." Sometimes a piece of a company can work better independently or be able to increase its market share. Sometimes it is more cost effective to have two separate companies. Most of the time spin-offs are companies started by good, solidly run companies. Maybe Coca-Cola wants to get into the orange juice business, or McDonalds decides to start another type of food chain. These are excellent spin-offs to play.

Spin-off companies can be put on your watch lists and periodically viewed for buy signals. You would usually buy a call on the "spinee," or the new company being spun off. Chances are in favor of the stock going up. Make sure and check the chart and the fundamentals (P/E).

3. CONTRACTS (FOR SERVICES OR JOINT VENTURE)

When a company receives a large order, do you think that could have an impact on the price of the stock? You bet.

How about Boeing selling airplanes. It's not uncommon to see one order in the $100 millions and often much more. This would tend to increase the price of the stock.

What if the news was a failed service contract? What would happen if a joint venture between two companies went awry? You could buy puts and expect the stock to go down.

4. NEW SERVICES OR PRODUCTS

Many announcements of new services or products can be good plays, especially if the chart and fundamentals look good. I've heard of people playing this strategy long before I knew what it was. People would get excited about making money based solely on a new product that a company was coming out with. It seems to me that they must have made some money using this strategy because they continued investing on news.

I do understand, however, that using Options on News, coupled with a good chart and a nice P/E, can sure increase your average (and maybe your yield).

5. DISASTER

This is not my favorite strategy, but you can make some good profits with really bad news. A disaster can be many things; a crashed airplane, a warehouse fire, flooding, earthquakes, and maybe a bankruptcy. Could a company going into or coming out of a bankruptcy have an affect on its stock? Yes.

A lot of disasters can be played with puts as the stock goes down and calls if the stock recovers from the disastrous news. Make sure you get good buy signals from the charts, and the fundamentals. Know the story of the company. What does it do? Why is the company having financial difficulty? Who is managing the company and how long have they been there? Does the company have assets to liquidate?

6. RECOVERY

This is specific news about a company that is recovering from recent events. Maybe the company was in bankruptcy, but was able to liquidate some asset, pay off debtors, and get back on track. This company is recovering.

Volatility here can be profitable. Find news about a company recovering and put it on your watch list. Maybe it will start a rolling pattern. Maybe it will trend upward with good support and resistance.

What we are playing in the context of this Option on News strategy is the little jump directly after the news. We don't necessarily care about the long-term consequences of the news. Other investors are responding to the news also, which has a tendency to drive the price of the stock, and therefore a magnified movement in the option.

Notes:

7. STOCK SPLIT

There are five specific entry points into this strategy. If you don't want to go into that detail, if that is not your style, you can still purchase calls on the news of a stock split. The news about stock splits will usually be Entry Point 1 or 2, the rumor or the announcement. It is my best suggestion that you Simutrade with news about stock splits using the Simutrade Worksheet for stock splits.

8. RUMOR

Rumors abound. There are rumors about possible stock splits, rumors of acquisitions, rumors about earnings, the list is unending. Remember: Buy on rumor, sell on news. If the rumor comes true, you would sell shortly thereafter. Don't get greedy. Just target for your little piece of profit. Don't go kill a tiger to satiate your hunger when you're in a vegetable garden.

The challenge is to find quality sources of rumors. Try CNBC. When I first got cable TV, I scanned all the channels. That was the last time I watched CNBC, until I started using the Options on News strategy. Now, I don't recommend that all of you turn on CNBC tonight for the market recap and news, but check it out sometime. If you know where to look when you want to find news, quality news services are the place to go. Investigate and explore a few and Simutrade the rumors. If they play out well, you may decide you like this strategy.

9. EARNINGS

Companies are always fixed on keeping track of what they are doing. Corporations must keep track of their accounting needs. Their accounting staff also forecasts the future by way of comparing to a historical past. You may see something like:

Tommy Hilfiger (TOM) reported earnings of .96 per share versus estimates .88. The company also announced that they would purchase two licensees owned by its officers for $1.15 billion in cash and stock. The stock closed at $43^9/_{16}.

If a company reports good earnings, this is seen as positive. Remember about P/E? The price of a stock usually follows the trend set by its earnings. Always pay close attention to earnings and the corresponding ratios.

Buy a call on good earnings. Buy a put on bad earnings. Check the charts and the fundamentals.

10. Stock Buy Backs

When a corporation views its stock as undervalued or at a wholesale price, they may think it's a good move for them to buy back their own stock. The verbiage is something like "...Directors agree to buy back up to 1,000,000 shares." Often, investors see the company's faith in itself, figure the company knows itself best, and they buy stock also. This combination drives the price up.

Again, what we are after here is to take advantage of the little jump in the stock as people act upon the news. Get our little hunk and get out.

11. Upgrades/Downgrades

This is a quaint little category of news. It seems to be very useful, however.

An Upgrade and a Downgrade are ratings by brokerage houses. Financial analysts study charts, fundamental analysis, technical analysis, financial reports, et cetera. They then rate the company's stock in comparison to other stocks. As the company changes, its rating can be upgraded or downgraded. Each brokerage house seems to have different terminology for their rating system, but the important thing to pay attention to here is the direction of the grade. If you have an upgrade, then you would want to buy calls. The good news should initiate a jump in the stock. This is positive news and the stock should go up. If you have a downgrade, people may decide to sell and the price of the stock may go down.

Notes:

Notes:

Here is an example:

6:44 AM Upgrades: Ceridian (CEN) to new buy at Credit Suisse First Boston, Micron Technologies (MU) to long term attractive at BancAmerica R.S., Federated Department Stores (FD) to outperform at Berntein.

Now, let's jump into some news. Again, I'm going to use an example of a pager system here. I believe that using a news source like a pager simplifies this strategy and gives me an advantage of getting the news early. I have more time to respond, and maybe collect information. When you do enough Simutrades, you will see the value in getting information quickly after the news is announced. If you target your little piece of profit, you're in a good position to succeed.

OPTIONS ON NEWS EXAMPLE 1

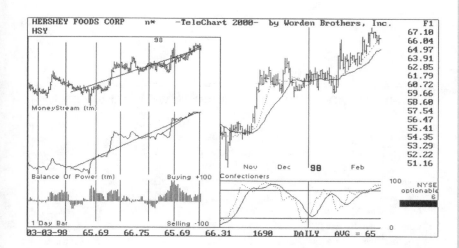

March 3, 1998

6:28 AM Upgrades: Hershey Foods (HSY) new buy at Credit Suisse First Boston

EVALUATION

This page came across IQ Pager™ at 6:28am. It took me awhile to get to the charts and fill out a Simutrade Worksheet. I decided to buy 10 March $65 Calls at 3⁷/₈. I calculated my 25% target profit and put in a GTC order to sell 10 at $4²⁷/₃₂. I was filled on the 9th for a profit of $968.75—25%.

Most news plays out pretty fast. I like to target my little chunk of profit, get in, and get out. Sometimes you can do this in a day, sometimes in a week. Is this risky? Yes. Can it be profitable? Again, yes. The more research you do the better informed you are to make a good decision.

Notes:

Notes:

SIMUTRADE OPTIONS/TRADING NEWS WORKSHEET

Date: __03/04/98__ Time: __1:00__   Broker: __Simutrade__

Company: __Hershey Foods__   Ticker: __HSY__ Quote: _____ X _$66^3/_{16}

P/E: _____   News: __Upgrade__

Notes: _____

Option: __Mar $65 Call__   Option Ticker: __SQXDH__ Quote: _____ X _$3^7/_8

Contracts Purchased: __10__   Price: _$3^7/_8

Exit Strategy: __25%. $3^7/_8 x 1.25 = $4.84375 = $4^{27}/_{32}__

Associated GTCs placed: __Sell 10 @ $4^{27}/_{32}__

Closing Trade: __10 @ $4^{27}/_{32}__ Date: __03/09/98__ Net Gain/Loss: __25%__

Price Graph: __+__	Balance of Power™: __+__	*Note:*
Stochastics: __o__	Volume: __+__	*Never act upon less than a three plus (+++) or a three minus (- - -) chart.*
MoneyStream™: __+/o__	Trend: __+__	
Total score for this chart: __+o++/++__		

Evaluation: _____

Cash Out:	$3^7/_8	=	$3.875	X 1,000 =	$3,875.00
Cash In:	$4^{27}/_{32}	=	$4.84375	X 1,000 =	$4,843.75
					$968.75 Gain

__$968.75 / $3,875 = 25% Gain__

OPTIONS ON NEWS EXAMPLE 2

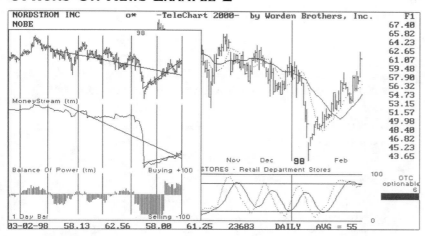

March 2, 1998

6:34 AM More Upgrades: Nordstrom (NOBE) to strong buy at Credit Suisse First Boston.

EVALUATION

This news came from IQ Pager™. It was an upgrade about Nordstrom. I checked the chart and did a little research and decided to buy 20 March $60 Calls for $2. I calculated my profit at 25% or $2¹/₂. I decided that I would target a little extra to see if I could get it. I placed two GTC orders: one for 10 at $2¹/₂ and one for 10 at $3¹/₂. I was filled at $2¹/₂ on 3/3 and my order for $3¹/₂ was filled a day later on the 4th. This gave me a profit of $2,000 or 50%. Based on this and other trades, maybe I could raise my target profit minimum on my Simutrade Game Plan Worksheet. Or, would that be greedy? I decided to stick to my 25%. I'm comfortable with 25% and have had good success with this target. You need to determine your target profit. Try a couple of different targets and do two Simutrades at the same time, one for one price and one for the other. See what happens.

Notes:

SIMUTRADE OPTIONS/TRADING NEWS WORKSHEET

Date: __03/02/98__ Time: ___1:00___   Broker: ___Simutrade___

Company: _Nordstrom_   Ticker: _NOBE_ Quote: ___ X _$61^1/4_

P/E: _____   News: _Upgrade_____

Notes: _____

Option: _Mar $60 Call_   Option Ticker: _NOQCL_ Quote: ___ X _$2_

Contracts Purchased: __20__   Price: _$2_

Exit Strategy: __25%. $2 x 1.25 = $2^1/2_____

Associated GTCs placed: __Sell 10 @ $2^1/2, Sell 10 @ $3^1/2_____

Closing Trade: _10@2^1/2,10@$3^1/2_ Date: __3-3/3-4___   Net Gain/Loss: __50%___

Price Graph: ___+___	Balance of Power™: ___+___	**Note:**
Stochastics: ___-___	Volume: _____+___	*Never act upon less*
MoneyStream™: _+_	Trend: _____+___	*than a three plus (+++)*
Total score for this chart: _+-++/++_		*or a three minus (- - -)*
		chart.

Evaluation: _____

Cash Out:	$2	=	$2.00	X 2,000 =	$4,000
Cash In:	$2^1/2	=	$2.50	X 1,000 =	$2,500
Cash In:	$3^1/2	=	$3.50	X 1,000 =	$3,500
					$2,000 Gain

__$2,000 / $4,000 = 50% Gain__

OPTIONS ON NEWS EXAMPLE 3

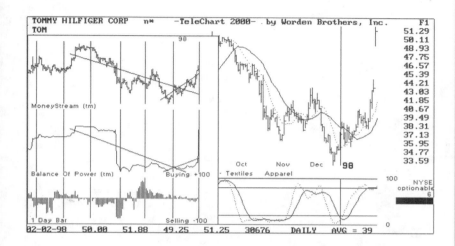

February 2, 1998

Upgrades: Tommy Hilfiger (TOM) raised to a 'buy' at DLJ and J.P. Morgan

EVALUATION

This example is from W.I.N.™ I was cruising the Net on W.I.N.™ and came across two new items about TOM. One was about a reported earnings increase and an announcement about the purchase of a license. The second was an upgrade to buy at two brokerages. I figured that this was double the news, so I tried it out.

I purchased 10 March $45 Calls for $6¹/₂. I calculated my 25% profit at $8¹/₈ and placed a GTC to sell all 10 at $8¹/₈. I was filled on the 6th for a profit of $1,625 or 25%. When I purchased the option, the price of the stock was about $44. Look at what TOM did over the next few days. Could I have gotten in again? Maybe. Could I have held on longer for more profit? Yes. But remember, stick to your game plan. I targeted 25% profit and I got it. This was a successful trade.

Notes:

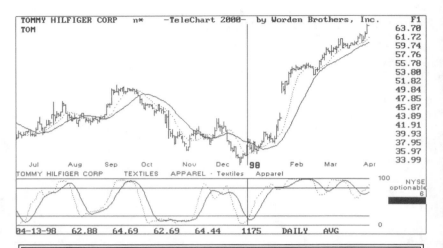

TOMMY HILFIGER CORP   n*   —TeleChart 2000— by Worden Brothers, Inc.   F1
TOM

```
63.70
61.72
59.74
57.76
55.78
53.80
51.82
49.84
47.85
45.87
43.89
41.91
39.93
37.95
35.97
33.99
```

Jul   Aug   Sep   Oct   Nov   Dec   '98   Feb   Mar   Apr

TOMMY HILFIGER CORP   TEXTILES   APPAREL · Textiles   Apparel

100   NYSE optionable 6

0

04-13-98   62.88   64.69   62.69   64.44   1175   DAILY   AVG

SIMUTRADE OPTIONS/TRADING NEWS WORKSHEET

Date: __02/02/98__ Time: __1:00__   Broker: __Simutrade__

Company: __Tommy Hilfiger__   Ticker: __TOM__ Quote: ____ X __43^9/_{16}$__

P/E: _____   News: __Upgrade/Earnings .96 vs .88/License__

Notes: _____

Option: __Mar $45 Call__   Option Ticker: __TOMCL__ Quote: ____ X __6^1/_2$__

Contracts Purchased: __10__   Price: __6^1/_2$__

Exit Strategy: __25%. 6^1/_2$ x 1.25 = 8.125 = 8^1/_8$__

Associated GTCs placed: __Sell 10 @ 8^1/_8$__

Closing Trade: 10 @ 8$^1/_8$ Date: __02/06/98__   Net Gain/Loss: __25%__

Price Graph: ___-___	Balance of Power™: ___+___	**Note:**
Stochastics: ___-___	Volume: ___+___	*Never act upon less*
MoneyStream™: ___+___	Trend: ___+___	*than a three plus (+++)*
Total score for this chart: __- - ++/++__		*or a three minus (- - -)*
		chart.

Evaluation: _____

Cash Out:	6^1/_2$	=	$6.50	X 1,000 = $6,500
Cash In:	8^1/_8$	=	$8.125	X 1,000 = $8,125
				$1,625 Gain

$1,625 / $6,500 = 25% Gain

OPTIONS ON NEWS EXAMPLE 4

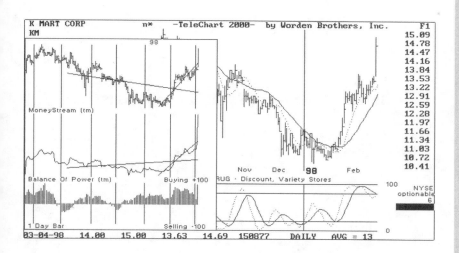

March 4, 1998

6:44 AM More Upgrades: Positive Earnings: Kmart (KM)

EVALUATION

This trade was from IQ Pager™ on March 4th. It was news of an upgrade. The chart looked good, so I decided to buy 20 contracts of the April $15 calls at $³/₄. I purchased 20 because of the low price. I calculated my 25% at $¹⁵/₁₆. Since I had 20 contracts, I placed two GTCs: one for 10 at $¹⁵/₁₆ and one for 10 at $1¹/₂ (double). I was filled on 3/5 for $¹⁵/₁₆ and on 3/9 for $1¹/₂. This gave me a cash profit of $937.50 or 62.5%.

I've heard of other investors targeting 100% on half of their position, thus breaking even, and letting the other half go up, up, up and trying to catch more of the trend. This is a little bold for my trading style. My game plan seems to be working for the style that I trade. Take time to fine-tune your game plan. It's okay to be different from others. Just find what works.

Notes:

SIMUTRADE OPTIONS/TRADING NEWS WORKSHEET

Date: __02/04/98__ Time: __1:00__   Broker: __Simutrade__

Company: __Kmart__   Ticker: __KM__   Quote: _____ X __$14^{11}/$_{16}$__

P/E: _____   News: __Positive Earnings__

Notes: _____

Option: __Apr $15 Call__   Option Ticker: __KMDC__   Quote: _____ X __$^{3}/$_4$__

Contracts Purchased: __20__   Price: __$^{3}/$_4$__

Exit Strategy: __25%. $^{3}/$_4$ x 1.25 = .9375 = $^{15}/$_{16}$__

Associated GTCs placed: __Sell 10 @ $^{15}/$_{16}$, Sell 10 @ $1^{1}/$_2$__

Closing Trade: __10@^{15}/$_{16}$, 10@1^{1}/$_2$__ Date: __3-5/3-9__   Net Gain/Loss: __62.5%__

Price Graph: ___+___ Balance of Power™: ___+___

Stochastics: ___-___ Volume: _____ +

MoneyStream™: _+_ Trend: _____ +

Total score for this chart: __+ - ++/++__

Note:
Never act upon less than a three plus (+++) or a three minus (- - -) chart.

Evaluation: _____

Cash Out:	$^{3}/$_4$	=	$.75	X 2,000 =	$1,500
Cash In:	$1^{1}/$_2$	=	$1.50	X 1,000 =	$1,500
Cash In:	$^{15}/$_{16}$	=	$.9375	X 1,000 =	$937.50

$937.50 Gain

$937.50 / $1,500 = 62.5% Gain

OPTIONS ON NEWS EXAMPLE 5

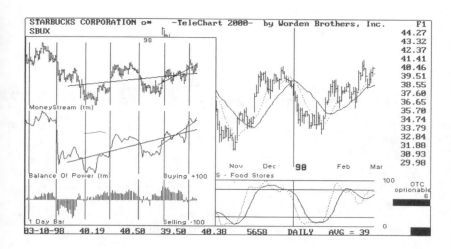

March 11, 1998

6:17 AM Upgrades: Starbucks (SBUX) to buy at Lehman Bros

EVALUATION

Playing Options on News seems easy when you have the right tools. IQ Pager™ qualifies as one of those tools that is useful. Take this example.

I got a page about an upgrade on Starbucks. I checked out the chart and it was okay. I decided to purchase 10 April $40 Calls for $2. I calculated my target profit of 25% and placed a GTC order to sell all 10 contracts at $2¹/₂. The next day the options gapped up above my GTC. I quickly canceled my GTC and placed an order to sell at $3¹/₄. I was filled shortly thereafter. This is a one-day profit of $1,250 or 62.5%!

Does a paging service work? I would answer, "Most Definitely!"

Notes:

SIMUTRADE OPTIONS/TRADING NEWS WORKSHEET

Date: __03/11/98__ Time: __1:00_____ Broker: __Simutrade_____

Company: __Starbucks_____ Ticker: __SBUX__ Quote: _____ X __$40³/₈__

P/E: _____ News: __Upgrade to buy_____

Notes: _____

_____

Option: __Apr $40 Call_____ Option Ticker: __SQXDH__ Quote: _____ X __$2__

Contracts Purchased: __10_____ Price: __$2__

Exit Strategy: __25%. $2 x 1.25 = $2¹/₂_____

Associated GTCs placed: __Sell 10 @ $2¹/₂_____

Closing Trade: __10 @ $3¹/₄____ Date: __03/12/98__ Net Gain/Loss: __62.5%____

Price Graph: ____+____ Balance of Power™: __o__ | **Note:**
Stochastics: ____o____ Volume: _____o__ | *Never act upon less*
MoneyStream™: __+____ Trend: _____+__ | *than a three plus (+++)*
Total score for this chart: __+o+o/o+____ | *or a three minus (- - -)*
  | *chart.*

Evaluation: _____

Cash Out: $2   = $2.00   X 1,000 = $2,000

Cash In: $3¹/₄   = $3.25   X 1,000 = $3,250

  $1,250 Gain

$1,250 / $2,000 = 62.5% Gain

	OPEN				STOCK TRANSACTION TRACKING RECORD					CLOSE					
Date	Stock	Price	B/S	Qty	Position	O/C	Ord	Fill $	Total	Date	B/S	Qty	Fill $	Total	Comms
3/4	HSY	66⁵/₁₆	B	10	Mar 65 P		1	3⁷/₈	3,875	3/9	S	10	4²⁷/₃₂	4,843.75	
Strategy	News				Notes					P/L $	968.75		Days	5 Yield 25.8 %	
2/2	NOBE	61¹/₄	B	20	Mar 60 C		2	2	4,000	3/3	S	10	2¹/₂	2,500	
Strategy					Notes					P/L $			Days	Yield %	
							2a			3/4	S	10	3¹/₂	3,500	
Strategy	News				Notes					P/L $	2,000		Days	2 Yield 50 %	
2/2	TOM	43⁹/₁₆	B	10	Mar 45 C		3	6¹/₂	6,500	2/6	S	10	8¹/₈	8,125	
Strategy	News				Notes					P/L $	1,625		Days	4 Yield 25 %	
3/4	KM	14¹¹/₁₆	B	20	Apr 15 C		4	³/₄	1,500	3/5	S	10	¹⁵/₁₆	937.50	
Strategy					Notes					P/L $			Days	Yield %	
							4a			3/9	S	10	1¹/₂	1,500	
Strategy	News				Notes					P/L $	937.50		Days	5 Yield 62.5 %	
3/11	SBUX	40³/₈	B	10	Apr 40 C		5	2	2,000	3/12	S	10	3¹/₄	3,250	
Strategy	News				Notes					P/L $	1,250		Days	1 Yield62.50 %	
Strategy					Notes					P/L $			Days	Yield %	
Strategy					Notes					P/L $			Days	Yield %	

Notes:

CHAPTER 14
Selling Naked Calls And Naked Puts

These two strategies will describe how to refine the buy low/sell high theory into an art form. We have already discussed selling calls in the chapter on Covered Calls and you should have a basic understanding of options on puts and calls from the Options chapter. If you need to review, I encourage you to do it now. It is important that you understand and are comfortable with terminology and concept for options. This will make trading easier. We'll also run through a couple of Simutrades at the end of this chapter.

In this strategy, we are going to introduce a new concept; going "Naked!" Sounds exciting doesn't it? Well, what you should really get excited about are all the benefits of being "naked" when selling puts or selling calls. The simple profits and strange returns will entice you.

The definition of selling naked options is simply the selling of an option on a stock that we don't own. Hence, the option is naked, or uncovered. These strategies entail us agreeing to buy (puts) or sell (calls) the stock at a specified strike price. By making this agreement or entering into this options contract, we will receive cash in our account in the form of a premium. We receive cash to sell the option at a current price and promise to buy/sell the stock at the strike price on expiration day.

Notes:

Selling Naked Puts and Selling Naked Calls are very similar. When you think the stock value will increase, you sell a put. Conversely, if you think the stock value will decrease, sell a call.

If you look at Entry Point 4 in the chapter on Stock Splits, for example, a put could be sold two or three days prior to the stock split pay date. Generally speaking, stocks will have a tendency to rise during the transition from the announcement to the pay date. We believe the stock to be rising so we sell a naked put.

You will want to be careful because sometimes stocks hit a price peak and decrease in value during a one-day trading period—the day of the stock split day. This scenario is similar for the announcement pattern of Entry Point 1 in the chapter on Stock Splits. In each case, when the stock hits a peak would be the time to sell a naked call. The selling of naked calls is done when the charts and evaluations indicate that the stock is at a peak and will go in a downward direction.

When you go searching for candidates for Selling Naked Puts, keep in mind that most stocks that are good covered call candidates will be great for Selling Naked Puts. The fundamentals are similar with covered calls. One might ask, "If this strategy falls in line with covered calls, why not use the covered call strategy?" We will look at the advantages of Selling Naked Puts and Calls; however, there are several hurdles one must conquer prior to being qualified to sell naked puts and calls.

Your ability to use this strategy depends on your brokerage house rules. Most firms have minimum account balances, minimum experience requirements in options, and maybe a few more rules just to be qualified to deal in naked options. My firm required that I have an account value of $25,000 or more and have a year of trading in options before they would let me start trading naked. Brokerage houses are so careful with naked options because if you have the stock put to you, you can lose a lot of money very quickly. For example, if you sell a naked put for $25 and the stock moves to $15, you will have to buy th stock at $25 and sell it at $15—that's a loss of $10 per share. You will have to check with your brokerage firm to see if you will quali-

SELLING NAKED CALLS AND NAKED PUTS

fy to use this strategy. I strongly recommend that before you risk any funds, you perfect your skills in this strategy by using the Simutrade System. Simutrade enough plays so that you feel comfortable and feel like you have mastered the techniques in the strategy. Then, if your broker has questions or wants verification of your ability to trade in naked options, show him your tracking records for this strategy and let him be the judge. It will at least show him that you are serious enough about not losing any money to take the time and effort to simulate actual trades. Simutrades count as experience in my book. If you can make money honestly Simutrading, you can make money with real cash trades.

There are several distinct advantages when you sell Naked Puts or sell Naked Calls. One major advantage is the margin requirements. Most brokerage houses only require 20 to 30 % of the stock's value that you wrote the option on for margin. This means instead of using 50% of the value of the stock price for margin when using the covered call strategy, you now can sell a Naked Call or Put, add instant cash to your account, and have the margin requirement significantly lower. This way you will have more free cash to trade with.

These strategies are truly about cash flow. They are good for generating new income. In addition, if the stock gets put to you or you get called out, you will be able to purchase the stock at a wholesale price by including the premium that you already received, your cash in. Since you may end up with stock, make sure that you only do deals with companies you would want to own. If you would not want to own the stock, don't "put" yourself in a position to own stock you don't want.

One of my favorite stocks that I have used with this strategy is a Northwest company, Eagle Hardware (EAGL). One day a friend of mine and I were conversing about our portfolios and he mentioned he was trading Eagle Hardware. I wanted to know how he was doing. He said, "Quite well."

I asked him what strategy he was using and he told me "Naked Puts." This got my attention. I had read the chapter in

Stock Market Miracles about selling naked puts but didn't fully understand the concept. I asked my friend to explain the details of his strategy so I could understand it better. After we were done, I went back to *Stock Market Miracles* and studied the information in light of this additional information.

I started Simutrading Eagle Hardware, and I had a lot of success. I felt confident enough to do real cash trades and contacted my broker. Since my account qualified for trading in naked positions, I started trading naked with Eagle Hardware.

I also noticed from the charts that this stock qualified and had the footprint of a rolling stock candidate.

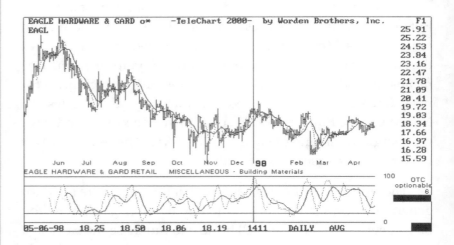

Let's dig into the strategy. First, we'll clarify the definitions for our positions. Stock option purchasing gives the investor the right, but not the obligation to buy or sell a stock at a set strike price on or before a certain date. Call options give the investor the right, not the obligation, to buy a stock. Put options give the investor the right, not the obligation, to sell a stock. These are normal options, if there is a norm. There is more buying of puts and calls than any other option strategy.

These put and call options can not only be purchased, they can be sold. If you sell a Naked Put, you are obligated to sell the stock at the strike price on the expiration date. If you were "put to," you would have to go purchase the stock at the current price and sell it at your strike price. Generally, if the price of the stock goes up, the value of the naked put goes up.

If you sell a Naked Call, it obligates you to sell the stock at the strike price, on the expiration date. If you are called out, you will purchase the stock at the strike price and own the stock.

For naked strategies, look for a stock that rolls up and down at least $2 to $3 frequently. When I looked at Eagle Hardware, I noticed that it ran from about $17 to $20. Check the W.I.N.™ for good naked put/call stock candidates. Do all the necessary gathering of information and fill out a Simutrade Worksheet. Check fundamentals and current news from *The Wall Street Journal* and your other sources of information. Do your analysis with the charts.

When selecting a stock, make sure you *really, really* like the company. The reasoning is simple; you might have to purchase the stock and would end up owning it. If you failed to do your research prior to your play, you might own a stock that does not fit within your game plan. I like to include fundamental targets to check for any stocks that I may wind up owning. Check the chart.

The upside of buying stocks after selling naked calls or puts is that you will be able to purchase the stock at a wholesale price. If you take the premium you received from the call or put and deduct it from the strike price, you come up with a cost basis that is less than the price of the stock, hence you're buying wholesale. If you receive a premium of $1.50 and your stock price is at $20, your cost basis would be $18.50 per share. I've heard of some people using this strategy to purchase stock that they want to own in order to receive a better price for it.

When you are Simutrading this strategy, you can choose to figure in your margin requirements. You can track the price of the stock and keep approximately 20 to 30% of this amount free in your account. Margin requirements can affect your ability to trade in real cash when the time comes. Use the Simutrading System to simulate your margin account as close to reality as possible.

Notes:

Notes:

SELLING NAKED PUTS

Once you have made your decision to sell a Naked Put, sell the next month out at the next lower strike price. As the stock value moves up closer to the strike price, the value of the option goes down. If the stock falls below the strike price, you may have the stock put to you. You can either accept the stock at the strike price or you could buy back your options. If there is sufficient time left before the expiration day, you may want to buy back your option at a reduced price, therefore locking in a profit. Remember, keep your "eye on the ball" while your position is open. If it is close to the expiration day and the stock price is above your strike price, you may just let the option expire as worthless. Either way, you are able to keep the premium that you collected originally.

If the stock moves down, however, you may want to buy back your option and close your position. Then you can explore reselling the same option on the next month out for another premium. You can also use GTC orders to sell your option at a specific price. Remember, you are selling first and buying second. Your GTC should be a buy order at a lower price than you sold so that you can lock in a smaller, but safe, profit.

SELLING NAKED CALLS

For Selling Naked Calls, you want to find a qualified candidate that is trading in a peak range and one that you expect to chart as a downward moving trend. Then sell a Naked Call; sell the next month out at the next higher strike price. Remember though, you have the obligation to sell the stock at the strike price if you get called out.

Remember the strategy basic to buy low and sell high? Well, Selling Naked Calls and Selling Naked Puts have this in reverse. We sell first when the call at the high peak of its range is at a good premium. When the stock price goes to or near your strike price that you sold the option for, the call option becomes of less value. At this time, you can make a decision to either buy the stock, let the option expire, or buy the option back. Sometimes the stock will go below your strike price and you must make decisions in a timely manner. Do your homework, watch the charts, and "keep your eye on the ball" when the time draws near for the options to expire.

As you become more experienced, you may want to sell Naked Puts on blue chip companies. To start out with, try and keep your costs low.

Notes:

SELLING NAKED PUTS EXAMPLE 1

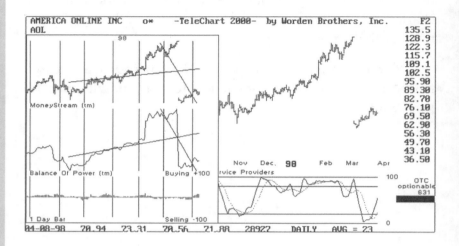

EVALUATION

Selling Naked Puts is risky, but fairly simple. I looked at the charts and some fundamentals and decided to sell May $70 Puts on AOL. I got a quote of 3\frac{1}{2}$. I sold the puts naked, and received a premium of $3,500. On the expiration day I was not exercised and got to keep my $3,500 premium.

Now, how do you calculate your yield when you have no cash out? Is it 100%, 1,000% or more? Well, you use your margin requirement in place of cash out. This is money that you are required to have in order to generate your gain. Simply take your strike price multiplied by the number of shares you control (100 per contract times the number of contracts) and then multiple by your margin factor. For the examples used in this book, 20% margin was used.

Notes:

SIMUTRADE SELLING PUTS WORKSHEET

Date: 04/08/98   Time: 1:00   Broker: Simutrade

Company: America Online Inc.   Ticker: AOL   Quote: _____ X 74^7/_8$

P/E: _____   News: None

Notes: Break even $70 minus 3^1/_2$ = 66^1/_2$

Option: May $70 Put _____ Option Ticker: AOLQN   Quote: 3^1/_2$ X _____

Contracts Sold: 10 _____ Price: 3^1/_2$

Associated GTCs placed: Stop 66^1/_2$

Closing Trade: Expired _____ Date: 04/17/98 ___ Net Gain/Loss: ___ 25%

Price Graph: ___+___ Balance of Power™: ___+___	**Note:**
Stochastics: ___+___ Volume: _____ + ___	*Never act upon less than a three plus (+++) or a three minus (- - -) chart.*
MoneyStream™: ___o___ Trend: _____ + ___	
Total score for this chart: ___++o+/++___	

Evaluation: _____

  Cash Out: $0   = $0.00   X 1,000 =   0

  Cash In: 3^1/_2$ = $3.50   X 1,000 = $3,500

                                                           $3,500 Gain

  Margin Requirement: Strike $170 x 1,000 = $70,000 x 20% margin = $14,000

  $3,500 / $14,000 = 25% Gain

SELLING NAKED PUTS EXAMPLE 2

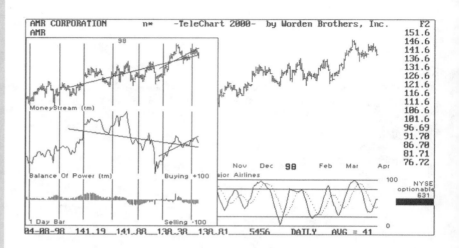

EVALUATION

This trade I did on the same day and in conjunction with the trade on AOL. The chart was good and I wrote 10 May $135 Puts for a premium of $3,500. On the 16th, the options were trading for about half of what I sold them for. I decided to lock in my profit and purchased 10 May $135 Puts to close out my position. On this trade I did things backwards. I sold high first, then purchased low. I made a profit of $1,750 at the end. You still use your margin requirement to calculate your rate of return, even though we have a cash out figure. Whether you let the option expire or buy it back you must have your margin requirement in your account and, therefore, use is to calculate your return.

SIMUTRADE SELLING PUTS WORKSHEET

Date: _04/08/98_   Time: _1:00_   Broker: _Simutrade_

Company: _AMR Corporation_   Ticker: _AMR_   Quote: _____ X $138^{13}/$_{16}$

P/E: _____   News: _None_

Notes: _Break even $135 minus $3^1/$_2$ = $131^1/$_2$_

Option: _May $135 Put_   Option Ticker: _AMRQG_   Quote: _$3^1/$_2$ X_

Contracts Sold: _10_   Price: _$3^1/$_2$_

Associated GTCs placed: _Stop $131^1/$_2$_

Closing Trade: _10 @ $1^3/$_4$_   Date: _04/16/98_   Net Gain/Loss: _6.5%_

Price Graph: _+_	Balance of Power™: _o_		**Note:**
Stochastics: _+_	Volume: _____		**Never act upon less**
MoneyStream™: _o_	Trend: _____		**than a three plus (+++)**
Total score for this chart: _++oo/oo_			**or a three minus (- - -)**
			chart.

Evaluation: _____

Cash Out:	$1^3/$_4$	=	$1.75	X 1,000 =	$1,750
Cash In:	$3^1/$_2$	=	$3.50	X 1,000 =	$3,500
					$1,750 Gain

Margin Requirement: Strike $135 x 1,000 = $135,000 x 20% margin = $27,000

$1,750 / $27,000 = 6.5% Gain

SELLING NAKED CALLS EXAMPLE 1

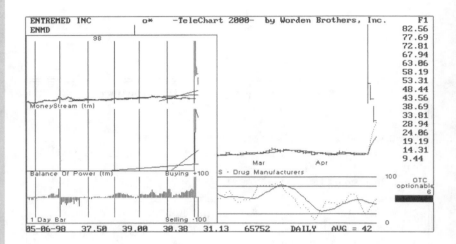

EVALUATION

If you look at the chart, ENMD did a unique thing. It had been trading in a range of $10 to $16 almost for-ever. Then, in one day, it jumped up over $80, and closed above $50. Talk about volatility. Do you think this stock is going to go up or down?

SIMUTRADE SELLING CALLS WORKSHEET

Date: 05/05/98   Time: 1:00   Broker: Simutrade

Company: Entremed Inc   Ticker: ENMD Quote: _____ X $43^9/$_{16}$

P/E:_____ News: None _____

Notes: Break even $50 minus $3^7/$_8$ = $46^1/$_8$ _____

Option: May $50 Call _____ Option Ticker: _____ Quote: $3^7/$_8$ X _____

Contracts Sold: 10 _____ Price: $3^7/$_8$ _____

Associated GTCs placed: Stop @ $46^1/$_8$ _____

Closing Trade: 10 @ $2^9/$_{16}$ _____ Date: 05/05/98 _____ Net Gain/Loss: 13.1% _____

Price Graph: ____+____ Balance of Power™: ____-____		**Note:**
Stochastics: ____+____ Volume: _____ +		*Never act upon less*
MoneyStream™: ____-____ Trend: _____ +		*than a three plus (+++)*
Total score for this chart: ___++ - - /++___		*or a three minus (- - -)*
		chart.

Evaluation: _____

    Cash Out: $2^9/$_{16}$ = $2.5625   X 1,000 = $2,562.50

    Cash In: $3^7/$_8$ = $3.875   X 1,000 = $3,875.00

                                                        $1,312.50 Gain

  Margin Requirement: Strike $50 x 1,000 = $50,000 x 20% margin = $10,000

  $1,312.50 / $10,000 = 13.1% Gain

Notes:

It is usually best to have a trend confirm itself before you get in. Make that one of the requirements on your game plan. If you look at the second chart below, you will see that it shows the Price Graph for the day of May 6th. Look at the dramatic price action from $39^1/$_8$ to $34^1/$_8$ in one day!

I sold 10 May $50 Calls at $3^7/$_8$ in the morning of the 5th. We were filled on our GTC to sell at $2^9/$_{16}$ that same day. This is a 13.1% profit in one day!

Be extremely careful while Selling Naked Calls. They are the most risky form of options that you can invest in. Your risk is unlimited, and your potential loss can go as high as the price of the stock can go. What would happen if you had purchased on the 1st or 2nd and found the price of your stock over $60 difference in one day? Again, be careful and Simutrade first, use real cash second.

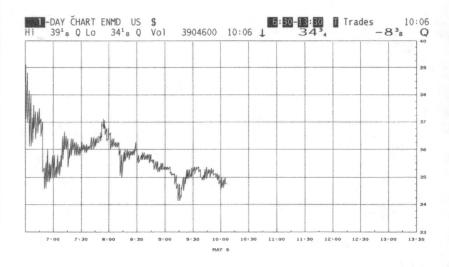

STOCK TRANSACTION TRACKING RECORD

	OPEN									CLOSE					
Date	Stock	Price	B/S	Qty	Position	O/C	Ord	Fill $	Total	Date	B/S	Qty	Fill $	Total	Comms
4/8	AOL	74 7/16	S	10	May 70 P		1	3 1/2	3,500			3.500		8	
Strategy	Naked Put				Notes					P/L $			Days	Yield	25%
4/8	AMR	81 13/16	S	10	May 135 P		2	3 1/2	3,500	4/16	B	10	1 3/4	1,750	
Strategy	Naked Put				Notes					P/L $		1,750	Days	8 Yield	6.5%
5/5	ENMD	43 9/16	S	10	May 50 C		1	3 7/8	3,875	5/5	B	10	2 9/16	2,562.50	
Strategy	Naked Call				Notes					P/L $	1,312.50		Days	1 Yield	13.1%
										P/L $			Days	Yield	%
Strategy					Notes					P/L $			Days	Yield	%
										P/L $			Days	Yield	%
Strategy					Notes					P/L $			Days	Yield	%
										P/L $			Days	Yield	%
Strategy					Notes					P/L $			Days	Yield	%
										P/L $			Days	Yield	%
Strategy					Notes					P/L $			Days	Yield	%
										P/L $			Days	Yield	%
Strategy					Notes					P/L $			Days	Yield	%

Notes:

CHAPTER 15

Bull Call And
Bull Put Spreads

The Bull Put Spread and the Bull Call Spread are combination strategies—you combine two strategies to make one. They are also considered a little more advanced because of the greater amount of information that you have to sift through. If you understand the strategies of puts and calls, then Simutrade some Bull Spreads and really experience how they work. Here are the basic strategies:

Bull Call Spread: Buy a call one month out with a lower strike price and sell a call one month out with a higher strike price.

Bull Put Spread: Sell a put one month out with a higher strike price and buy a put one month out with a higher strike price.

The "Bull" is the indication that we want the trend of the stock to be up. We want our moving averages on the rise with the shorter on top. This is a "Bullish" strategy and is best used in a "Bull" market.

One way to look at what we are doing in spreads is to compare it to the "middle man," someone who purchases at wholesale, adds a little markup, and sells to retail distributors. That little markup in the middle is our Spread—the difference between what we buy for and what we sell for. In Bull Spreads

Notes:

187

we are shopping for a good difference between the option that we sell and the option that we buy. We also need to factor in the difference between the strike price in case we hold on to the options and they are exercised.

BULL CALL SPREAD

The Bull Call Spread is like an older brother of the covered call. One problem with writing covered calls is the amount of cash that you may have tied up from purchasing the stock. Would it scare you to calculate how much a covered call would be on a company like Microsoft? It may take all of your available cash and a loan on your house.

Well, with Spreads you can and should invest in solid companies like Microsoft. That is one advantage to Spreads—we get to invest in premium blue chip companies without using all of our cash. You can move into a better neighborhood of companies. You see, instead of purchasing the stock like you do with a covered call, you are purchasing a call. If the stock is above your strike price at expiration, you will get called out. The call that you purchased can be substituted instead of owning the stock. It's called a Same Day Substitution (SDS) and can only happen with calls. When you have a Same Day Substitution you will be charged an additional set of commissions. The Bull Call Spread entails four trades and four commissions. I've heard that some people have negotiated a lower commission on their trades with Bull Call Spreads. Would it hurt to ask your broker?

Check the chart, check the fundamentals, and then shop for a good spread. You sell a call (the right to have someone call the stock away from you) and buy a call (the right to call the stock away from someone else), so your profit is the difference between the two. Instead of purchasing the stock like you do in covered calls, you substitute with buying calls.

Search for a spread of $1 to $1³/₄ (or 12 to 18%). You will find that the spread is always a negative number. You buy a call for $8 and sell a call for $5. This leaves you $3 per share that makes up your cash out. So, how do you make a profit? By getting called out. If you buy an $80 call and sell an $85 call, when you are exercised, you have a capital gain of $5 per share. Subtract from this our negative spread of $3 and you have a profit of $2. That is the basic target scenario.

Find a spread and go shopping for the options. One of the most crucial things is to buy options that are below the current price of the stock. These options may be more expensive, but they make this strategy safer. If the price of the stock stays well above your upper strike price, you will be called out and realize our maximum profit. If the price of the stock falls below your strike price, you will not get called out. If you hold on to your options, you may lose up to 100% at expiration. Or, you could choose to "unwind" our spread.

Unwinding is just closing out our position. Instead of a simple sell or buy, we have to sell the option that we purchased and buy the option that we sold. In essence, we sell one spread for another. If the price of the stock goes below our strike price and we don't get called out, we are going to lose money. I say target your loss and pay special attention to it when the price of the stock starts getting close to our strike price. If the spread goes down enough for us to meet our target loss, pull the trigger, let the arrow go, and get out of the trade.

This strategy is bullish and therefore relies on the price of the stock going up. Stock split candidates can also be good candidates for Bull Call Spreads.

When your are searching for a Bull Call Spread, keep some paper handy. Some spreads will work and some won't. Once you find one that you think will work, write it down on the Simutrade Worksheet. Always check your spread. The art of spreads is in shopping for good deals. Shop around and try a bunch of different numbers. Some numbers will work and some won't. When you find a spread that looks good, check and see if you have a buy signal from the chart and fundamentals. If everything looks good and conforms to your game plan, grab your Simutrade Worksheet and complete it.

Notes:

Notes:

Practice this strategy. Then practice it some more. At first glance, this strategy may seem confusing. The terminology can be confusing because they are so close to each other—buying a call and selling a call. Be dedicated in following the steps, and fill out some Simutrades. You should get the hang of it fairly quickly.

BULL PUT SPREAD

One difference between a Bull Call Spread and a Bull Put Spread is the way you exit the spread. With a Bull Call Spread you have a negative spread—you end up having money on the line until you get called out. With a Bull Put Spread you get a positive spread and have money in your pocket right away. If you wait and let the options expire, you get to keep the premiums. You produce a good, quick cash flow and have not a dime of your cash tied up.

With a Bull Put Spread you buy a put and sell a put. You receive a premium for selling the put and pay to purchase a put. This strategy is like Selling Naked Puts. One problem with Selling Naked Puts is that you have to have part of your cash tied up for margin. Although it is only approximately 30% of the stock value, selling 10 puts of an $80 stock can tie up around $24,000.

There is no Same Day Substitution on Bull Put Spreads. If the stock stays above your strike prices, both puts will expire worthless and you keep the premium. This is what you want to have happen.

If the stock price drops, you need to be concerned with the puts that you sold. You have an obligation to perform on your option if it is a put to you. You can buy back the puts that you sold and close out your position. If you do this, you may have to give back a small portion of your premium profit. Or, you can buy back your option and roll it out to the next month.

Nearly everyone can be approved to do Bull Call Spreads. Talk to your broker and ask him specifically about Bull Call

Spreads. Practice Simutrading Bull Call Spreads so that you can get the hang of it. It has been my experience that certain investors latch onto Bull Spreads, especially Bull Put Spreads and refine it into their favorite strategy. This strategy is great for carving out small chunks of profit and it produces an almost instant cash flow—you receive the premiums in your account the next day.

Let's look at what we are doing firsthand by filling out a few Simutrade Worksheets and looking at the corresponding charts.

Notes:

BULL CALL SPREAD EXAMPLE 1

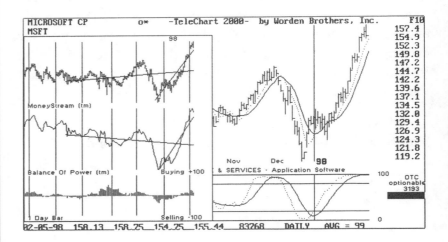

EVALUATION

Here, we have a good solid uptrend in place. MSFT has also announced a stock split. We have a debit spread of -$7¹/₄ ($7,250 cash out). When we get called out, we will get $10,000 cash in, minus the cash out of $7,250, equals a profit of $2,750. This is a 27.5% rate of return.

On the ex-date of March 20, the price of the stock was above $81 (remember, this is after the split, so it is actually $162), we get called out, and we realize our 27.5% profit.

SIMUTRADE BULL CALL SPREAD WORKSHEET

Date: 02/05/98   Time: 1:00   Broker: Simutrade

Company: Microsoft   Ticker: MSFT   Quote: _____ X $155⁷/₁₆

P/E: _____   News: _____

Notes: _____

Option to Buy: Mar $150 Call   Option Ticker: MSQCJ   Quote: _____ X $9³/₈

Option to Sell: Mar $160 Call   Option Ticker: MSQCL   Quote: $2¹/₈ X _____

Contracts Purchased: 10   Price: $9³/₈

Contracts Sold: 10   Price: $2¹/₈

Exit Strategy: _____

Associated GTCs placed: _____

Closing Trade(s): Called Out   Date: 02/20/98

Called Out   Date: 02/20/98   Net Gain/Loss: 27.5%

Price Graph: o	Balance of Power™: +	**Note:**
Stochastics: o	Volume: +	*Never act upon less*
MoneyStream™: o	Trend: +	*than a three plus (+++)*
Total score for this chart: ooo+/++		*or a three minus (- - -)*
		chart.

Evaluation: _____

Cash Out:	$9³/₈	=	$9.375	X 1,000 =	$9,375
Cash In:	$2¹/₈	=	$2.125	X 1,000 =	$2,125
			Net Cash Out (Debit Spread)	$7,250

Cash Out:		$150	X 1,000 =	$150,000
Cash In:		$160	X 1,000 =	$160,000
		Net Cash In (Exercised)	$10,000

$10,000 Cash In minus $7,250 Cash Out = $2,750 Gain

Margin Requirement = $160 - $150 x 1,000 = $10,000

$2,750 / $10,000 = 27.5% Gain

Notes:

BULL CALL SPREAD EXAMPLE 2

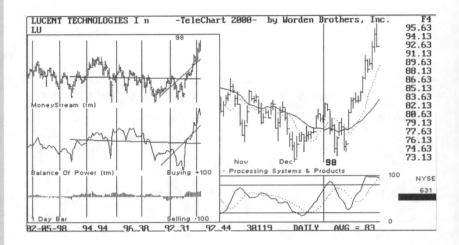

EVALUATION

Lucent is another stock split candidate. If something works, I like to stick with it. Stock splits work well with bullish strategies. We've got a -4^{13}/_{16}$ debit spread ($4,812.5 cash out). When we get called out, we have $10,000 additional cash in for capital gains, so our profit is $5,187.50. On the ex-date, the price of the stock is $60+ (or $120 accounting for the split). This is well above our strike prices and we get called out. This is a nice trade.

SIMUTRADE BULL CALL SPREAD WORKSHEET

Date: 02/05/98   Time: 1:00   Broker: Simutrade

Company: Lucent Technologies   Ticker: LU   Quote: _____ X 92^7/_{16}$

P/E: _____   News: _____

Notes: _____

Option to Buy: Mar $90 Call Option Ticker: LUCR   Quote: _____ X 6^7/_8$

Option to Sell: Mar $100 Call Option Ticker: LUCT   Quote: 2^1/_{16}$ X _____

Contracts Purchased: 10   Price: 6^7/_8$

Contracts Sold: 10   Price: 2^1/_{16}$

Exit Strategy: _____

Associated GTCs placed: _____
_____

Closing Trade(s): Called Out   Date: 02/20/98

                 Called Out   Date: 02/20/98   Net Gain/Loss: 51.9%

Price Graph: o	Balance of Power™: +	**Note:**
Stochastics: o	Volume: +	*Never act upon less*
MoneyStream™: -	Trend: +	*than a three plus (+++)*
Total score for this chart: oo - +/++		*or a three minus (- - -)*
		chart.

Evaluation:

Cash Out:	6^7/_8$	= $6.875	X 1,000 =	$6,875.00
Cash In:	2^1/_{16}$	= $2.0625	X 1,000 =	$2,062.50
		Net Cash Out (Debit Spread)		$4,812.50

Cash Out:	$90	X 1,000 =	$90,000
Cash In:	$100	X 1,000 =	$100,000
	Net Cash In (Exercised)		$10,000

$10,000 Cash In minus $4,812.50 Cash Out = $5,187.50 Gain

Margin Requirement = $100 - $90 x 1,000 = $10,000

$5,187.50 / $10,000 = 51.9% Gain

Notes:

BULL CALL SPREAD EXAMPLE 3

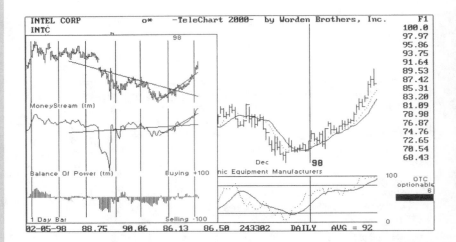

EVALUATION

Intel has a good chart. We have a debit spread of $2³/₈ ($2,625 cash out). This means that when I get called out, I receive $5,000 for capital gains. This creates a potential profit of $2,375, or 47.5%. The stock on ex-date was just where I wanted it to be, so I realized a 47.5% profit.

SIMUTRADE BULL CALL SPREAD WORKSHEET

Date: 02/05/98   Time: 1:00   Broker: Simutrade

Company: Intel   Ticker: INTC   Quote: $87 $^{11}/_{16}$ X $87 $^{3}/_{4}$

P/E: _____   News: _____

Notes: _____

Option to Buy: Feb $85 Call   Option Ticker: INQBQ   Quote: _____ X $6

Option to Sell: FEb $90 Call   Option Ticker: INQBR   Quote: $3 X _____

Contracts Purchased: 10   Price: $5 $^{5}/_{8}$

Contracts Sold: 10   Price: $3

Exit Strategy: _____

Associated GTCs placed: _____

Closing Trade(s): Called Out   Date: 02/20/98

Called Out   Date: 02/20/98   Net Gain/Loss: 47.5%

Price Graph: o	Balance of Power™: o	**Note:**	
Stochastics: o	Volume: +	*Never act upon less*	
MoneyStream™: +	Trend: +	*than a three plus (+++)*	
Total score for this chart: oo+o/++		*or a three minus (- - -)* *chart.*	

Evaluation: _____

Cash Out:	$5 $^{5}/_{8}$	= $5.625	X 1,000 =	$5,625
Cash In:	$3	= $3.00	X 1,000 =	$3,000
		Net Cash Out (Debit Spread)		$2,625

Cash Out:	$85	X 1,000 =	$85,000
Cash In:	$90	X 1,000 =	$90,000
	Net Cash In (Exercised)		$5,000

$5,000 Cash In minus $2,625 Cash Out = $2,375 Gain

Margin Requirement = $90 - $80 x 1,000 = $5,000

$2,375 / $5,000 = 47.5% Gain

BULL PUT SPREAD EXAMPLE 1

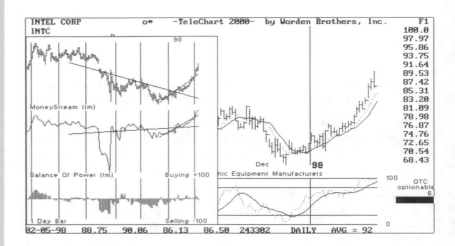

EVALUATION

Since Bull Call Spreads and Bull Put Spreads are bullish—you're looking for the same buy signals—this example goes along with the previous Simutrade.

We have a spread of $\$^{11}/_{16}$ ($687.50 cash in). The price of the stock kept an upward trend, although there was one dip. The options expired on the ex-date and I got to keep the premiums. My cash out was $312.50 from buying the puts, and my cash in was $1,000. To calculate our return, we take our cash in of $687.50 and divide it by our margin requirement of $5,000 ($85 strike price minus $80 strike price times 100 shares per contract times 10 contracts) to arrive at a 13.7% return.

Notes:

SIMUTRADE BULL PUT SPREAD WORKSHEET

Date: __02/05/98__   Time: __1:00__   Broker: __Simutrade__

Company: __Intel__   Ticker: __INTC__   Quote: _____ X $87⁵/₄

P/E: _____   News: _____

Notes: _____

Option to Buy: __Feb $80 Put__   Option Ticker: __INQNP__   Quote: _____ X $⁵/₁₆

Option to Sell: __Feb $85 Put__   Option Ticker: __INQNQ__   Quote: __$1__   X _____

Contracts Purchased: __10__   Price: $⁵/₁₆

Contracts Sold: ____10____   Price: __$1__

Exit Strategy: _____

Associated GTCs placed: _____

Closing Trade(s): __Expired__   Date: __02/20__

__Expired__   Date: __02/20__   Net Gain/Loss: ___13.7%___

			Note:
Price Graph: __o__	Balance of Power™: __o__		*Never act upon less*
Stochastics: __o__	Volume: _____ +		*than a three plus (+++)*
MoneyStream™: __+__	Trend: _____ +		*or a three minus (- - -)*
Total score for this chart: __oo+o/++__			*chart.*

Evaluation: _____

Cash Out:	$⁵/₁₆	=	$.3125	X 1,000 =	$312.50
Cash In:	$1	=	$1.00	X 1,000 =	$1,000.00
			Net Cash In (Credit Spread)		$687.50

Margin Requirement = $85 - $80 x 1,000 = $5,000

$687.50 / $5,000 = 20% Gain

Notes:

BULL PUT SPREAD EXAMPLE 2

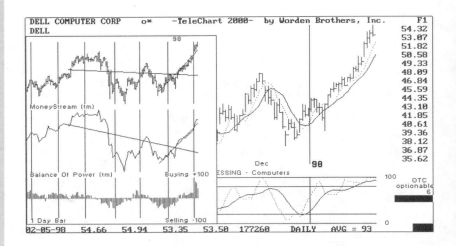

EVALUATION

Here is a good chart with a solid uptrend in place. Again, this stock has announced a stock split. We get a credit spread of $1 ($1,000 cash in). The trend continues to our ex-date of 2/20 and our puts expire worthless, with $2,062.50 total cash in and $1,062.50 cash out. Again, to get our return we take our net credit of $1,000 and divide by the money that it took to create this amount, our margin requirement of $5,000 to arrive at a 20% return. Not bad at all.

SIMUTRADE BULL PUT SPREAD WORKSHEET

Date: __02/05/98__   Time: __1:00_____   Broker: __Simutrade_____

Company: __Dell Computer_____   Ticker: __DELL__ Quote: _____ X __$109____

P/E: _____   News: _____

Notes: _____

_____

Option to Buy: __Feb $100 Put__ Option Ticker: __DLQNT__ Quote: _____ X $$1^1/_{16}$$

Option to Sell: __Feb $105 Put__ Option Ticker: __DLQNA__ Quote: $$\$2^1/_{16}$$ X _____

Contracts Purchased: __10_____   Price: $$\$1^1/_{16}$$

Contracts Sold: _____10_____   Price: $$\$2^1/_{16}$$

Exit Strategy: _____

Associated GTCs placed: _____

_____

Closing Trade(s): __Expired_____   Date: __02/20_____

_____ __Expired_____   Date: __02/20_____   Net Gain/Loss: __20%_____

Price Graph: __o__	Balance of Power™: __+__	Note:
Stochastics: __o__	Volume: __+__	Never act upon less than a three plus (+++) or a three minus (- - -) chart.
MoneyStream™: __+__	Trend: __+__	
Total score for this chart: __oo++/++__		

Evaluation: _____

Cash Out:	$$\$1^1/_{16}$$	=	$1.0625	X 1,000 =	$1,062.50
Cash In:	$$\$2^1/_{16}$$	=	$2.0625	X 1,000 =	$2,062.50
		Net Cash In (Credit Spread)			$1,000.00

_____

__Margin Requirement = $105 - $100 x 1,000 = $5,000_____

__$1,000 / $5,000 = 20% Gain_____

Notes:

STOCK TRANSACTION TRACKING RECORD

	OPEN									CLOSE					
Date	Stock	Price	B/S	Qty	Position	O/C	Ord	Fill $	Total	Date	B/S	Qty	Fill $	Total	Comms
2/5	MSFT		B	10	Mar 150 C		1	$9\frac{3}{8}$	9,375	2/20	B	1000	150	150,000	%
Strategy Bull Call Spread				Notes						P/L $	2,750		Days		Yield 27.5%
			S	10	Mar 160 C		1a	$2\frac{1}{8}$	2,125	2/20	S	1000	160	160,000	
2/5	LU		B	10	Mar 90 C		2	$6\frac{7}{8}$	6,875	2/20	B	1000	90	90,000	%
Strategy Bull Call Spread				Notes						P/L $	5,187.50		Days		Yield 51.9%
			S	10	Mar 100 C		2a	$2\frac{1}{16}$	2,062.50	2/20	S	1000	100	100,000	
2/5	INTC	$87\frac{3}{4}$	B	10	Feb 85 C		3	$5\frac{5}{8}$	5,625	2/20	B	1000	85	85,000	%
Strategy Bull Call Spread				Notes						P/L $	2,375		Days		Yield 47.5%
			S	10	Feb 90 C		3a	3	3,000	2/20	S	1000	90	90,000	
2/5	DELL	109	B	10	Feb 100 P		5	$1\frac{1}{16}$	1,062.50						%
Strategy Naked Put				Notes						P/L $		1,000	Days		Yield 20%
			S	10	Feb 105 P		5a	$2\frac{1}{16}$	2,062.50						
Strategy				Notes						P/L $			Days		%

CHAPTER 16

LEAPS®

LEAPS® (Long Term Equity Anticipation Securities) are options that have a longer time frame attached to them. Instead of a normal option that will expire in less than six months, LEAPS® are written for up to two years out. Most of the time you will only find LEAPS® on large, solid, blue-chip type companies. This allows you to play big name companies for long-term trades without tying up the large amounts of cash that it would take to purchase the stock. *The Wall Street Journal* has a section that lists the companies offering LEAPS®. The name of the strategy describes just exactly what you are looking for the stock to do. The word anticipation in the name is what you hope or predict the stock will do in the future.

One of the best uses for LEAPS® is Entry Point 5 in the chapter on Stock Splits, the post split play. If we look at larger companies that split on a regular basis, you will notice that they have a certain pattern. Usually one or more splits per year can happen. The price of the stock has a tendency to drift back up to the price before the split. This pattern usually takes from nine months to over a year.

Since we can predict with some accuracy that the stock will split, wouldn't it be nice to capitalize on this trend? You bet! What would happen if we used LEAPS® to capitalize on a long-term period of a company that historically does stock splits?

Notes:

Notes:

Throughout this book we have encouraged you to diversify your portfolio. In risky investments it is extremely important for you to only invest money that you can afford to lose without damaging your portfolios. In my opinion, LEAPS® fall into the category of safe investments, if there is such a thing. If you like good blue chip stock and have enough time and money to wait for the predictable to happen, the LEAPS® strategy may be the vehicle for you.

After reading W.I.N.™ and Wade Cook's explanation of LEAPS®, I decided to try it on Micosoft (MSFT). I have used this strategy in my long-term game plan, but recently the options have grown so dramatically that I have bought and sold them twice on my January 1999 position. Here is the information that I found on W.I.N.™ You be the judge.

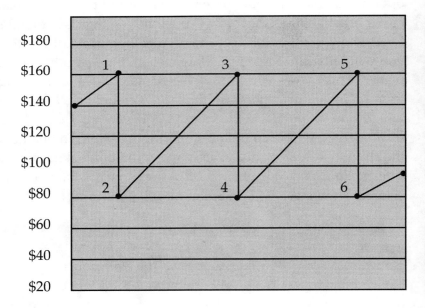

We will only use intrinsic value—the difference between the price of the stock and our strike price—to simplify our example. Needless to say, the numbers shown are underestimated until the expiration date.

Notes:

Buy 10 contracts of Jan 2000 $200 Calls at $20:

1	MSFT	Strike	Contracts	Cost	Value	Mkt Value
	$160	$200	10	$20	$20	$20,000

Stock splits 2 for 1 down to $80:

2	MSFT	Strike	Contracts	Cost	Value	Mkt Value
	$80	$100	20	$10	$10	$20,000

Assume that the stock price rises back to $160. The LEAPS will increase by to $60:

3	MSFT	Strike	Contracts	Cost	Value	Mkt Value
	$160	$100	20	$10	$60	$120,000

Then, if stock splits 2 for 1 again:

4	MSFT	Strike	Contracts	Cost	Value	Mkt Value
	$80	$50	40	$5	$30	$120,000

Assume if the stock again rises from $80 to $160:

5	MSFT	Strike	Contracts	Cost	Value	Mkt Value
	$160	$50	40	$5	$110	$440,000

Then if it splits for a third time:

6	MSFT	Strike	Contracts	Cost	Value	Mkt Value
	$80	$25	80	$2.5	$55	$440,000

After reviewing the information, I decided to play the January 1999 $100 call options on Microsoft. I purchased two contracts for $5 each. My total out of pocket cash was $1,000. I had planned to let them ride either to expiration date or, if the premiums got high enough, I would sell them. A couple of weeks ago, I was browsing W.I.N.™ and noticed that Wade was selling some of his positions on Microsoft. The stock was around $98 that day and the January 1999 $100s were about $12. I decided that I would sell at a handsome profit. I had purchased the options for $5 about a month and a half before. I sold them that morning for a profit of $7 each.

The stock then started to fade back down towards the $90 range. When the option price for the same calls I had sold for $12 was reduced to $8.50, I purchased three contracts with the original money I had, plus my profits from the first sale. The option price then went to about $7.25. Maybe I should have waited to see if it had truly hit its low, but I am satisfied with all that I have done on this play so far.

I am convinced that Microsoft is an outstanding, predictable company and will perform historically as shown on the graphs. Since I am obligating a fair amount of cash on this one play I am in the process of Simutrading the other examples that I found on W.I.N.™ By Simutrading these other plays on Microsoft I will have a chance to observe this stock and the strategy performance. I may decide to adjust my course and my game plan. Then I will trade with real money. Since I am already profitable on my first trade, Simutrading will help me retain the profits and fulfill my needs to feel good about the trade.

In the above example from W.I.N.™, if you were to purchase $20,000 worth of LEAPS® they would be worth over $440,000 before they expire. If you research Microsoft you will notice that they have had a split at least once a year for the last eight or nine years. Do you think that this trend is going to continue in the future? I'd put money on it and buy LEAPS®.

THE
RESOURCES

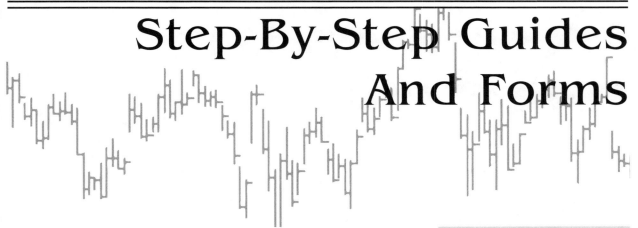

APPENDIX 1
Step-By-Step Guides And Forms

After receiving my pilot's license I decided to take my wife for an airplane ride. Once we completed the walk-around inspection, we climbed into the cockpit and proceeded with the step-by-step checklist. About halfway through the checklist, my wife suddenly opened the door. She said, "If you need an instruction manual to know how to fly this machine, you can go alone." When I explained to her that the checklist was a method or a step-by-step reminder that covers all procedures to successfully fly the airplane with a minimum amount of mistakes, she conceded to get back in and we had a wonderful time. The material in this appendix is a recap of the step-by-step guides and forms that go with them. They are very useful and will assist you in the Simutrading process. Use them in conjunction with your game plan. The trading checklist will make you successful in implementing your game plan.

Notes:

SIMUTRADE GAME PLAN WORKSHEET

Starting Point: _____ Date: _____

Destination/Goal: _____

_____

Portfolio Allotment: _____

_____

Trade Allotment: _____

_____

Time Temperament: _____

_____

Strategy(ies): _____

_____

_____

Entry Requirements

Chart: _____ Volume: _____Trend:_____

P/E: _____ Check News:_____

Exit Requirements

Moving Averages: _____ Target Loss: _____

Target Profit: _____

Sources for candidates: _____

_____

_____

_____

_____

Notes: _____

_____

_____

_____

_____

STOCK CANDIDATE LIST

Ticker	Price	Strategy	P/E	PG	S	BP	MN	V	T	=

Stock Transaction Tracking Record

OPEN									CLOSE							
Date	Stock	Price	B/S	Qty	Position	O/C	Ord	Fill $	Total	Date	B/S	Qty	Fill $	Total	Comms
Strategy				Notes						P/L $			Days	Yield	%
Strategy				Notes						P/L $			Days	Yield	%
Strategy				Notes						P/L $			Days	Yield	%
Strategy				Notes						P/L $			Days	Yield	%
Strategy				Notes						P/L $			Days	Yield	%
Strategy				Notes						P/L $			Days	Yield	%
Strategy				Notes						P/L $			Days	Yield	%
Strategy				Notes						P/L $			Days	Yield	%
Strategy				Notes						P/L $			Days	Yield	%

ROLLING STOCKS

1. THE STRATEGY

    a. Find a stock which channels between a high and low range from 25¢ to $5.

    b. Identify the entry point (support).

    c. Identity the exit point (resistance).

    d. Buy 1,000 shares or more at the entry point.

    e. Place a GTC order to sell at the exit point.

    f. When the GTC is filled at the exit point, place an order to buy the stock at the same entry point as before.

2. THE STEPS

    a. Gather Information

        • Check W.I.N.™ for stock candidates.

        • Get the company fundamentals (P/E).

        • Always check for any current news.

    b. Analyze

        • Stochastics: lines crossing at the bottom 0 to 20% lines and heading up.

        • Price Graph: at or near the bottom of recent price range.

        • MoneyStream™: uptick.

        • Balance of Power™: turning positive, red to yellow to green.

    c. Act

        • Do it.

           Simutrade or real trade

        • Don't do it—Look for a better deal!

SIMUTRADE ROLLING STOCKS WORKSHEET

Date:_____ Time:_____ Broker: _____

Company: _____ Ticker:_____ Quote:_____ X_____

Entry Point (Support Level): _____ Exit Point (Resistance Level):_____

Shares Purchased: _____ Price:_____

Notes: _____

_____

Associated GTCs placed: _____

_____

Closing Trade: _____ Date: _____ Net Gain/Loss: _____

Price Graph:_____ Balance of Power™: _____

Stochastics: _____ Volume: _____

MoneyStream™:_____ Trend: _____

Total score for this chart: _____

Note:
*Never act upon less
than a three plus (+++)
or a three minus (- - -)
chart.*

Evaluation: _____

_____

_____

_____

_____

_____

_____

_____

_____

_____

_____

_____

_____

BUYING CALLS

1. THE STRATEGY

   a. Find a stock that is going up.

   b. Buy a call (nearest strike price in the money or out of the money, next one to three months out for short-term, or three to twelve months out for long-term).

   c. Sell the call when the stock moves up.

   d. Don't be greedy!

2. THE STEPS

   a. Gather Information
      - Check W.I.N.™ for stock candidates.
      - Get the company fundamentals (P/E).
      - Always check for any current news.

   b. Analyze
      - Stochastics: lines crossing at the bottom 0 to 20% lines and heading up.
      - Price Graph: at or near the bottom of recent price range.
      - MoneyStream™: uptick.
      - Balance of Power™: turning positive, red to yellow to green.

   c. Act
      - Do it.

        Simutrade or real trade
      - Don't do it—Look for a better deal!

SIMUTRADE BUYING CALLS WORKSHEET

Date: _____ Time: _____ Broker: _____

Company: _____ Ticker: _____ Quote: _____ X _____

P/E: _____ News: _____

Notes: _____

_____

Option: _____ Option Ticker: _____ Quote: _____ X _____

Contracts Purchased: _____ Price: _____

Exit Strategy: _____

Associated GTCs placed: _____

_____

Closing Trade: _____ Date: _____ Net Gain/Loss: _____

Price Graph: _____ Balance of Power™: _____   **Note:**

Stochastics: _____ Volume: _____   *Never act upon less*

MoneyStream™: _____ Trend: _____   *than a three plus (+++)*

Total score for this chart: _____   *or a three minus (- - -)*
    chart.

Evaluation: _____

_____

_____

_____

_____

_____

_____

_____

_____

_____

_____

_____

_____

_____

_____

BUYING PUTS

1. THE STRATEGY

   a. Find a stock which is going down in value.

   b. Buy a put (as close to at the money as possible, and with two to three months of time).

   c. Sell the put when the stock moves down.

2. THE STEPS

   a. Gather Information

      - Check W.I.N.™ for stock candidates.

      - Get the company fundamentals (P/E).

      - Always check for any current news.

   b. Analyzing

      - Stochastics: lines crossing at the upper 80 to 100% lines and heading down.

      - Price Graph: at or near the top of recent price range.

      - MoneyStream™: downtick.

      - Balance of Power™: turning negative from green to yellow to red.

   c. Act

      - Do it.

        Simutrade or real trade

      - Don't do it—Look for a better deal!

SIMUTRADE BUYING PUTS WORKSHEET

Date:_____ Time:_____ Broker:_____

Company: _____ Ticker: _____ Quote: _____ X _____

P/E: _____ News: _____

Notes: _____

_____

Option: _____ Option Ticker:_____ Quote:_____ X _____

Contracts Purchased: _____ Price: _____

Exit Strategy: _____

Associated GTCs placed: _____

_____

Closing Trade: _____ Date: _____ Net Gain/Loss: _____

Price Graph:_____ Balance of Power™: _____		**Note:**
Stochastics: _____ Volume: _____		*Never act upon less*
MoneyStream™:_____ Trend: _____		*than a three plus (+++)*
		or a three minus (- - -)
Total score for this chart: _____		*chart.*

Evaluation: _____

_____

_____

_____

_____

_____

_____

_____

_____

_____

_____

_____

_____

_____

COVERED CALLS

1. THE STRATEGY

a. Buy stock ($5 to $25 range).

b. Sell call (next month, next higher strike price).

c. Let calls expire (or get called out).

Either:

- Rewrite calls for next month, or
- Sell stock and move on to a better play.

2. THE STEPS

a. Gather Information

- Check W.I.N.™ for stock candidates.
- Get the company fundamentals (P/E).
- Always check for any current news.

b. Analyze

- Stochastics: lines crossing at the bottom 0-20% lines and heading up.
- Price Graph: at or near the bottom of recent price range.
- MoneyStream™: uptick.
- Balance of Power™: turning positive, red to yellow to green.

c. Act

- Do it.

Simutrade or real trade

- Don't do it—Look for a better deal!

SIMUTRADE COVERED CALLS WORKSHEET

Date: _____ Time: _____ Broker: _____

Company: _____ Ticker: _____ Quote: _____ X _____

P/E: _____ News: _____

Notes: _____

_____

Option: _____ Option Ticker: _____ Quote: _____ X _____

Shares Purchased: _____ Price: _____

Contracts Sold: _____ Price: _____

Associated GTCs placed: _____

_____

Closing Trade: _____ Date: _____ Net Gain/Loss: _____

Price Graph: _____ Balance of Power™: _____   *Note:*

Stochastics: _____ Volume: _____   *Never act upon less*

MoneyStream™: _____ Trend: _____   *than a three plus (+++)*
or a three minus (- - -)
Total score for this chart: _____   *chart.*

Evaluation: _____

_____

_____

_____

_____

_____

_____

_____

_____

_____

_____

_____

_____

_____

_____

STOCK SPLITS

1. THE STRATEGY

   a. Historically
      - Find stocks that split on a regular basis.
      - Look for clues in the charts or in corporate announcements.

   b. When the stock split is announced
      - Act immediately!
      - Follow the big money!

   c. Post split announcement
      - Wait for profit taking after the good new.
      - Look for DUCks before buying.

   d. Pay-date split play
      - Wait until the pay date or two to three days before to buy.
      - Hold options through the split date, one to three days maximum.

   e. Post stock split play
      - Watch for the longer term DUCks play to buy.
      - Buy longer term options.

2. THE STEPS

   a. Gather Information
      - Check W.I.N.™ for stock candidates.
      - Get the company fundamentals (P/E).
      - Always check for any current news.

   b. Analyze

      For stock splits many of these rules may not apply.
      - Stochastics: lines crossing at the bottom 0 to 20% lines and heading up.
      - Price Graph: at or near the bottom of recent price range.
      - MoneyStream™: uptick.
      - Balance of Power™: turning positive, red to yellow to green.

   c. Act
      - Do it.

        Simutrade or real trade
      - Don't do it—Look for a better split deal!

SIMUTRADE STOCK SPLITS WORKSHEET

Strategy: _____
(Preannouncement, Announcement, Post Announcement, DUCk, et cetera)

Date: _____ Time: _____ Broker: _____

Company: _____ Ticker: _____ Quote: _____ X _____

Split Date: _____ Split Ratio: _____

Option: _____ Option Ticker: _____ Quote: _____ X _____

Notes: _____
_____

Contracts Purchased: _____ Price: _____

Exit Strategy: _____

Associated GTCs placed: _____
_____

Closing Trade: _____ Date: _____ Net Gain/Loss: _____

Price Graph: _____ Balance of Power™: _____   *Note:*

Stochastics: _____ Volume: _____   *Never act upon less*
than a three plus (+++)
MoneyStream™: _____ Trend: _____   *or a three minus (- - -)*
chart.
Total score for this chart: _____

Evaluation: _____
_____
_____
_____
_____
_____
_____
_____
_____
_____
_____
_____
_____
_____
_____
_____

STOCK SPLITS

1. HISTORICAL ANALYZING

    Buy stocks that traditionally split at certain price levels every year or two.

    a. Watch for annual shareholders meetings or Board of Directors meetings.

    b. Watch for shareholder notices to increase the number of shares by 50 to 100%.

    c. Watch potential candidates for "price gaps." These indicate news leaks and insider trading before announcements are made to the public.

    d. Reliable rumors of a stock split are often tradeable.

2. THE "INSTANT" THE SPLIT IS ANNOUNCED

    When a stock split is announced during market hours it is often possible to take advantage of the first few hours' up-move. On a big stock, the move will often last one to three days before the price settles back from profit taking.

    RULES FOR IMMEDIATE ACTION:

    a. Act immediately after the announcement. Five to ten minutes can mean the difference of several points. Watch out for stale news.

    b. Follow the big money. Play the big well-known corporations.

    c. If available, check the charts for favorable price patterns. Prior "gaps" to the upside are good indicators of investor interest.

3. POST SPLIT ANNOUNCEMENT

    Three to 10 days after the split announcement, the stock often shows a pattern of pulling back. At this point one has a second opportunity to take advantage of the stock split announcement. Buy the DUCks (Dipping Undervalued Calls).

    a. Watch the chart patterns to confirm
        *   The pullback, and
        *   The turn back to the upside.

    b. Often there are three to four of these opportunities before the actual split date.

    c. Look for prior highs to use as a get-out point.

4. "PAY DATE" SPLIT PLAY - "THE DUCK TAIL"

This play gets you into the stock options the day before the split. This play historically has high odds of profit.

a. Watch the stock pattern the week of the stock split "pay date." The pattern should be up, or in the worst case, sideways.

b. Hold the option through the split (you now have twice as many options). Selling them at your original cost equals a 100% gain!

c. Sell the options within three days of the split.

d. Buy the closest month "out of the money" call.

e. Don't be greedy!

f. Use common sense! If the stock is crashing one or two days before the "pay date" do not play the game. Wait for another train to come by. Don't get hit by this one.

5. POST STOCK SPLIT PLAY

Big stocks that are most recognized by the trading institutions and the public most often return to their old pre-split highs. They are usually the leaders in their industry group. Stocks that split have a 250% greater chance of going up than those that do not split.

a. Watch the charts for a long dip and profit taking before buying long term "in the money" options.

b. Stocks can be purchased on margin and out of the money calls written to collect premiums, with a high potential to be "called out" with a capital gain.

c. Look for the DUCks play.

PEAKS AND SLAMS

1. THE STRATEGY

   a. Find a stock that has just recently jumped up or been slammed 5 to 25% (one to three hours to one to three days).

   b. Buy the nearest in the money option with the nearest month.

      Peaks:

      • Buy Puts.

      Slams:

      • Buy Calls.

   c. Place GTC order quickly for fast profit.

   d. Don't be greedy.

2. THE STEPS

   a. Gather Information

      • Check W.I.N.™ for stock candidates.

      • Get the company fundamentals (P/E).

      • Always check for any current news.

   b. Analyze

      • Stochastics: the move is too fast to follow with any usefulness.

      • Price graph: at or near the top of recent price range for Peaks.

      • MoneyStream™: downtick for Peaks, uptick for Slams.

      • Balance of Power™: Peaks—turning negative from green to yellow to red and Slams—turning negative from red to yellow to green.

   c. Act

      • Do it.

         Simutrade or real trade

      • Don't do it—Look for a better deal!

SIMUTRADE PEAKS AND SLAMS WORKSHEET

Date: _____ Time: _____ Broker: _____

Company: _____ Ticker: _____ Quote: _____ X _____

P/E: _____ News: _____

Notes: _____

_____

Option: _____ Option Ticker: _____ Quote: _____ X _____

Contracts Purchased: _____ Price: _____

Exit Strategy: _____

Associated GTCs placed: _____

_____

Closing Trade: _____ Date: _____ Net Gain/Loss: _____

Price Graph: _____ Balance of Power™: _____

Stochastics: _____ Volume: _____

MoneyStream™: _____ Trend: _____

Total score for this chart: _____

Note:
Never act upon less than a three plus (+++) or a three minus (- - -) chart.

Evaluation: _____

_____

_____

_____

_____

_____

_____

_____

_____

_____

_____

_____

_____

_____

OPTION/TRADING NEWS

1. THE STRATEGY

   Look for news of:

   a. Acquisitions (Buy the company being acquired.)

   b. Spin-offs

   c. Contracts/joint ventures

   d. New services/products

   e. Disasters

   f. Recovery

2. THE STEPS

   a. Gather Information
      - Check W.I.N.™ for stock candidates.
      - Get the company fundamentals (P/E).
      - Always check for any current news.

   b. Analyze
      - Stochastics: for a buy-lines crossing at the bottom 0 to 20% lines and heading up; for a sell-lines crossing at the top 80 to 100% lines and heading down.
      - Price Graph: at or near the bottom of recent price range.
      - MoneyStream™: uptick (buy) or downtick (sell).
      - Balance of Power™: for a buy-turning positive, red to yellow to green; for a sell-turning negative from green to yellow to red.

   c. Act
      - Do it.

        Simutrade or real trade
      - Don't do it—Look for a better deal!

SIMUTRADE OPTIONS/TRADING NEWS WORKSHEET

Date: _____ Time: _____ Broker: _____

Company: _____ Ticker: _____ Quote: _____ X _____

P/E: _____ News: _____

Notes: _____

_____

Option: _____ Option Ticker: _____ Quote: _____ X _____

Contracts Purchased: _____ Price: _____

Exit Strategy: _____

Associated GTCs placed: _____

_____

Closing Trade: _____ Date: _____ Net Gain/Loss: _____

Price Graph: _____ Balance of Power™: _____	*Note:*
Stochastics: _____ Volume: _____	*Never act upon less*
MoneyStream™: _____ Trend: _____	*than a three plus (+++)*
Total score for this chart: _____	*or a three minus (- - -)*
	chart.

Evaluation: _____

_____

_____

_____

_____

_____

_____

_____

_____

_____

_____

_____

_____

_____

_____

SELLING CALLS

1. THE STRATEGY

   a. Find a stock that is going down in value.

   b. Sell a call (next higher strike price, next month out).

   c. When the stock moves down
      - Buy call back at a reduced price, or
      - Let call expire as worthless.

   d. If the stock moves up
      - Buy back call on expiration date and
      - Resell same option next month out for a greater premium.

2. THE STEPS

   a. Gather Information
      - Check W.I.N.™ for stock candidates.
      - Get the company fundamentals (P/E).
      - Always check for any current news.

   b. Analyze
      - Stochastics: lines crossing at the top 100 to 80% lines and heading down.
      - Price Graph: at or near the top of recent price range.
      - MoneyStream™: downtick.
      - Balance of Power™: turning negative, green to yellow to red.

   c. Act
      - Do it.

        Simutrade or real trade
      - Don't do it—Look for a better deal!

SIMUTRADE SELLING CALLS WORKSHEET

Date:_____ Time:_____ Broker:_____

Company:_____ Ticker:_____ Quote:_____ X_____

P/E:_____ News:_____

Notes:_____

_____

Option:_____ Option Ticker:_____ Quote:_____ X_____

Contracts Sold:_____ Price:_____

Associated GTCs placed:_____

_____

Closing Trade:_____ Date:_____ Net Gain/Loss:_____

Price Graph:_____ Balance of Power™: _____

Stochastics: _____ Volume: _____

MoneyStream™:_____ Trend: _____

Total score for this chart: _____

Note:
Never act upon less than a three plus (+++) or a three minus (- - -) chart.

Evaluation:_____

_____

_____

_____

_____

_____

_____

_____

_____

_____

_____

_____

_____

SELLING PUTS

1. THE STRATEGY

   a. Find a stock that is going up in value.

   b. Sell a put (next lower strike price, next month out).

   c. When the stock moves up
      - Buy put back at a reduced price, or
      - Let put expire as worthless.

   d. If the stock moves down
      - Buy back put on expiration date and
      - Resell same option next month out for a greater premium.

2. THE STEPS

   a. Gather Information
      - Check W.I.N.™ for stock candidates.
      - Get the company fundamentals (P/E).
      - Always check for any current news.

   b. Analyze
      - Stochastics: lines crossing at the bottom 0 to 20% lines and heading up.
      - Price Graph: at or near the bottom of recent price range.
      - MoneyStream™: uptick.
      - Balance of Power™: turning positive, red to yellow to green.

   c. Act
      - Do it.

        Simutrade or real trade
      - Don't do it—Look for a better deal!

SIMUTRADE SELLING PUTS WORKSHEET

Date:_____ Time:_____ Broker:_____

Company:_____ Ticker:_____ Quote:_____X_____

P/E:_____ News:_____

Notes:_____

_____

Option:_____ Option Ticker:_____ Quote:_____X_____

Contracts Sold:_____ Price:_____

Associated GTCs placed:_____

_____

Closing Trade:_____ Date:_____ Net Gain/Loss:_____

Price Graph:_____ Balance of Power™:_____

Stochastics:_____ Volume:_____

MoneyStream™:_____ Trend:_____

Total score for this chart:_____

Note:
Never act upon less than a three plus (+++) or a three minus (- - -) chart.

Evaluation:_____

_____

_____

_____

_____

_____

_____

_____

_____

_____

_____

_____

_____

_____

BULL CALL SPREAD

1. THE STRATEGY

   a. This is a way to, in effect, write a covered call on a higher priced stock

   b. Buy a deep in the money call option and sell an at the money call option on a stock on a dip that has started trending up.

   c. The stock moves up, and at expiration, both options are exercised, closing the position.

2. THE STEPS

   a. Gather Information

      - Check W.I.N.™ for stock candidates.
      - Get the company fundamentals (P/E).
      - Always check for any current news.
      - You are looking for options that would allow you to buy a lower strike price call and sell a higher strike price call for a debit which will allow a 10% or greater return when the options are exercised.

   b. Analyze

      - Check option chains for candidates. If you are looking at a stock that is $97, look at $90 and $95 options.
      - Stochastics: lines crossing at the bottom 0 to 20% lines and heading up.
      - Price Graph: at or near the bottom of recent price range.
      - MoneyStream™: uptick.
      - Balance of Power™: turning positive, red to yellow to green.

   c. Act

      - Do it.

        Simutrade or real trade
      - Don't do it—Look for a better deal!

SIMUTRADE BULL CALL SPREAD WORKSHEET

Date:_____ Time:_____ Broker:_____

Company: _____ Ticker:_____ Quote:_____ X_____

P/E:_____ News:_____

Notes:_____

_____

Option to Buy: _____ Option Ticker:_____ Quote:_____ X_____

Option to Sell: _____ Option Ticker:_____ Quote:_____ X_____

Contracts Purchased: _____ Price:_____

Contracts Sold: _____ Price:_____

Exit Strategy:_____

Associated GTCs placed:_____

_____

Closing Trade(s): _____ Date:_____

_____ Date:_____ Net Gain/Loss:_____

Price Graph:_____ Balance of Power™:_____   **Note:**
Stochastics:_____ Volume:_____   *Never act upon less*
MoneyStream™:_____ Trend:_____   *than a three plus (+++)*
Total score for this chart: _____   *or a three minus (- - -)*
chart.

Evaluation: _____

_____

_____

_____

_____

_____

_____

_____

_____

_____

_____

_____

_____

_____

BULL PUT SPREAD

1. THE STRATEGY

    a. Sell a deep in-the-money put option and buy an at-the-money put option on a stock on a dip that has started trending up.

    b. The stock moves up, and at expiration, both options expire, closing the position.

2. THE STEPS

    a. Gather Information
       - Check W.I.N.™ for stock candidates.
       - Get the company fundamentals (P/E).
       - Always check for any current news.
       - You are looking for options that would allow you to sell a higher strike price put and buy a lower strike price put for a credit which will allow a 10% or greater return when the options expire.

    b. Analyzing
       - Check option chains, looking for candidates.
       - Stochastics: lines crossing at the bottom 0 to 20% lines and heading up.
       - Price Graph: at or near the bottom of recent price range.
       - MoneyStream™: uptick.
       - Balance of Power™: turning positive, red to yellow to green.

    c. Act
       - Do it.

         Simutrade or real trade
       - Don't do it—Look for a better deal!

SIMUTRADE BULL PUT SPREAD WORKSHEET

Date: _____ Time: _____ Broker: _____

Company: _____ Ticker: _____ Quote: _____ X _____

P/E: _____ News: _____

Notes: _____

_____

Option to Buy: _____ Option Ticker: _____ Quote: _____ X _____

Option to Sell: _____ Option Ticker: _____ Quote: _____ X _____

Contracts Purchased: _____ Price: _____

Contracts Sold: _____ Price: _____

Exit Strategy: _____

Associated GTCs placed: _____

_____

Closing Trade(s): _____ Date: _____

_____ Date: _____ Net Gain/Loss: _____

Price Graph: _____ Balance of Power™: _____   *Note:*
Stochastics: _____ Volume: _____   *Never act upon less*
MoneyStream™: _____ Trend: _____   *than a three plus (+++)*
Total score for this chart: _____   *or a three minus (- - -)*
chart.

Evaluation: _____

_____

_____

_____

_____

_____

_____

_____

_____

_____

_____

_____

_____

_____

APPENDIX 2
Available Resources

The following books, videos, and audiocassettes have been reviewed by the Wade Cook Seminars, Inc. or Lighthouse Publishing Group, Inc. staff and are suggested as reading and resource material for continuing education to help with your financial planning, and real estate and stock market investments. Because new ideas and techniques come along and laws change, we're always updating our catalog.

To order a copy of our current catalog, please write or call us at:

Wade Cook Seminars, Inc.
14675 Interurban Avenue South
Seattle, Washington 98168-4664
1-800-872-7411

Or, visit us on our websites at:
www.wadecook.com
www.lighthousebooks.com

Also, we would love to hear your comments on our products and services, as well as your testimonials on how these products have benefited you. We look forward to hearing from you!

AUDIOCASSETTES

13 FANTASTIC INCOME FORMULAS—A FREE CASSETTE
Presented by Wade B. Cook

Learn 13 cash flow formulas, some of which are taught in the Wall Street Workshop™. Learn to double some of your money in $2^1/_2$ to 4 months.

ZERO TO ZILLIONS
Presented by Wade B. Cook

A four-album, 16-cassette, powerful audio workshop on Wall Street—understanding it, playing it successfully, and retiring rich. Learn 11 powerful investment strategies as you drive. Learn to avoid pitfalls and losses. Learn to catch "day-trippers" and how to "bottom fish." Learn to write covered calls and to possibly double your money in one week on options on stock split companies. Wade "Meter Drop" Cook can teach you how he makes 300% per year in his accounts. You then will have the information to try to follow suit. Each album comes with a workbook, and the entire workshop includes a free bonus video called "Dynamic Dollars," 90 minutes of instruction on how all the strategies can be integrated, and giving actual examples of what kinds of returns are possible so you can get in there and play the market successfully. A must for every savvy, would-be investor.

POWER OF NEVADA CORPORATIONS—A FREE CASSETTE
By Wade B. Cook

Nevada Corporations have secrecy, privacy, minimal taxes, no reciprocity with the IRS, and protection for shareholders, officers, and directors. This is a powerful seminar.

INCOME STREAMS—A FREE CASSETTE
By Wade B. Cook

Learn to buy and sell real estate the Wade Cook way. This informative cassette will instruct you in building and operating your own real estate money machine.

MONEY MACHINE I & II
By Wade B. Cook

Learn the benefits of buying and ,more importantly, selling real estate. Now the system for creating and maintaining a real estate money machine is available in audiocassette form. Money Machine I & II teach the step-by-step cash flow formulas that made Wade Cook and thousands like him millions of dollars.

MONEY MYSTERIES OF THE MILLIONAIRES—A FREE CASSETTE
By Wade B. Cook

How to make money and keep it. This fantastic seminar shows you how to use Nevada Corporations, Living Trusts, Pension Plans, Charitable Remainder Trusts, and Family Limited Partnerships to protect your assets.

24 KARAT
Presented by Wade B. Cook

Learn how to protect your family's finances through anything—including Y2K! 24 Karat seminar on cassette teaches people how currency fluctuates and the safest currency to have. This seminar is packed with must-know information about your future.

UNLIMITED WEALTH AUDIO SET
By Wade B. Cook

Unlimited Wealth is the "University of Money-Making Ideas" home study course that helps you improve your money's personality. The heart and soul of this seminar is to make more money, pay fewer taxes, and keep more for your retirement and family. This cassette series contains the great ideas from *Wealth 101* on tape, so you can listen to them whenever you want.

RETIREMENT PROSPERITY
By Wade B. Cook

Take that IRA money now sitting idle and invest it in ways that generate you bigger, better, and quicker returns. This four audiotape set walks you through a system of using a self directed IRA to create phenomenal profits, virtually tax free! This is one of the most complete systems for IRA investing ever created.

THE FINANCIAL FORTRESS HOME STUDY COURSE
By Wade B. Cook

This eight-part series is the last word in entity structuring. It goes far beyond mere financial planning or estate planning. It helps you structure your business and your affairs so that you can avoid the majority of taxes, retire rich, escape lawsuits, bequeath your assets to your heirs without government interference, and, in short, bomb-proof your entire estate. There are six audio cassette seminars on tape, an entity structuring video, and a full kit of documents.

PAPER TIGERS AND PAPER CHASE
By Wade B. Cook

Wade gives you a personal introduction to the art of buying and selling real estate. In this set of six cassettes, Wade shares his inside secrets to establishing a cash flow business with real estate investments. You will learn how to find discounted second mortgages, find second mortgage notes and make them better, as well as how you can get 40%-plus yields on your money. Learn the art of structuring your business to attract investors and bring in the income you desire through the use of family corporations, pension plans, and other legal entities. A manual is included.

When you buy Paper Tigers, you'll also receive Paper Chase for free. Paper Chase holds the most important tools you need to make deals happen. Wade created these powerful tapes as a handout tool you can lend to potential investors or homeowners to help educate them about how this amazing cash flow system works for them. It explains how you'll negotiate a lower interest rate if they make a larger payment. You will use this incredible tool over and over again.

THE REAL ESTATE CASH FLOW SYSTEM
Presented by Wade B. Cook

This six-volume audiocassette set, originally sold separately, contains everything you'll ever need to begin investing in real estate immediately, do so successfully, handle all of the business aspects and retire sooner than you ever thought possible. Just look at all the tremendous information that can be yours.

BOOKS

WALL STREET MONEY MACHINE
By Wade B. Cook

Appearing on the *New York Times Business Best-Sellers List* for over one year, *Wall Street Money Machine* contains the best strategies for wealth enhancement and cash flow creation you'll find anywhere. Throughout this book, Wade Cook describes many of his favorite strategies for generating cash flow through the stock market: Rolling Stock, Proxy Investing, Covered Calls, and many more. It's a great introduction for creating wealth using the Wade Cook formulas.

STOCK MARKET MIRACLES
By Wade B. Cook

The anxiously-awaited partner to *Wall Street Money Machine*, this book is proven to be just as invaluable. *Stock Market Miracles* improves on some of the strategies from *Wall Street Money Machine*, as well as introduces new and valuable twists on our old favorites. This is a must read for anyone interested in making serious money in the stock market.

BEAR MARKET BALONEY

By Wade B. Cook

A more timely book wouldn't be possible. Wade's predictions came true while the book was at press! Don't miss this insightful look into what makes bull and bear markets and how to make exponential returns in any market.

ROLLING STOCKS

By Gregory Witt

Rolling Stocks shows you the simplest and most powerful strategy for profiting from the ups and downs of the stock market. You'll learn how to find rolling stocks, get in smoothly at the right price, and time your exit. You will recognize the patterns of rolling stocks and how to make the most money from these strategies. Apply Rolling Stocks principles to improve your trading options and fortify your portfolio.

SLEEPING LIKE A BABY

By John C. Hudelson

Perhaps the most predominant reason people don't invest in the stock market is fear. *Sleeping Like A Baby* removes the fear from investing and gives you the confidence and knowledge to invest wisely, safely, and profitably.

You'll learn how to build a high quality portfolio and plan for your future and let your investments follow. Begin to invest as early as possible, and use proper asset allocation and diversification to reduce risk.

THE SECRET MILLIONAIRE GUIDE TO NEVADA CORPORATIONS

By John V. Childers Jr.

What does it mean to be a secret millionaire? In *The Secret Millionaire Guide To Nevada Corporations*, attorney John V. Childers Jr. outlines exactly how you can use some of the secret, extraordinary business tactics used by many of today's super-wealthy to protect your assets from the ravages of lawsuits and other destroyers using Nevada Corporations. You'll understand why the state of Nevada has become the preferred jurisdiction for those desiring to establish corporations and how to utilize Nevada Corporations for your financial benefit.

MILLION HEIRS

By John V. Childers Jr.

In his reader-friendly style, attorney John V. Childers Jr. explains how you can prepare your loved ones for when you pass away. He explains many details you need to take care of right away, before a death occurs, as well as strategies for your heirs to utilize. Don't leave your loved ones unprepared—get *Million Heirs*.

REAL ESTATE MONEY MACHINE
By Wade B. Cook

Wade's first bestselling book reveals the secrets of Wade Cook's own system—the system he earned his first million from. This book teaches you how to make money regardless of the state of the economy. Wade's innovative concepts for investing in real estate not only avoids high interest rates, but avoids banks altogether.

HOW TO PICK UP FORECLOSURES
By Wade B. Cook

Do you want to become an expert money maker in real estate? This book will show you how to buy real estate at 60¢ on the dollar or less. You'll learn to find the house before the auction and purchase it with no bank financing—the easy way to millions in real estate. The market for foreclosures is a tremendous place to learn and prosper. *How To Pick Up Foreclosures* takes Wade's methods from *Real Estate Money Machine* and supercharges them by applying the fantastic principles to already-discounted properties.

COOK'S BOOK ON CREATIVE REAL ESTATE
By Wade B. Cook

Make your real estate buying experiences profitable and fun. *Cook's Book On Creative Real Estate* will show you how! You will learn suggestions for finding the right properties, buying them quickly, and profiting even quicker.

OWNER FINANCING
By Wade B. Cook

This is a short but invaluable booklet you can give to sellers who hesitate to sell you their property using the owner financing method. Let this pamphlet convince both you and them. The special report, "Why Sellers Should Take Monthly Payments," is included for free!

REAL ESTATE FOR REAL PEOPLE
By Wade B. Cook

A priceless, comprehensive overview of real estate investing, this book teaches you how to buy the right property for the right price, at the right time. Wade Cook explains all of the strategies you'll need and gives you 20 reasons why you should start investing in real estate today. Learn how to retire rich with real estate, and have fun doing it.

101 Ways To Buy Real Estate Without Cash
By Wade B. Cook

Wade Cook has personally achieved success after success in real estate. *101 Ways To Buy Real Estate Without Cash* fills the gap left by other authors who have given all the ingredients but not the whole recipe for real estate investing. This is the book for the investor who wants innovative and practical methods for buying real estate with little or no money down.

Blueprints for Success, Volume 1
Contributors: Wade Cook, Debbie Losse, Joel Black, Dan Wagner, Tim Semingson, Rich Simmons, Greg Witt, JJ Childers, Keven Hart, Dave Wagner and Steve Wirrick

Blueprints for Success, Volume 1 is a compilation of chapters on building your wealth through your business and making your business function successfully. The chapters cover education and information gathering, choosing the best business for you from all the different types of businesses, and a variety of other skills necessary for becoming successful. Your business can't afford to miss out on these powerful insights!

Brilliant Deductions
By Wade B. Cook

Do you want to make the most of the money you earn? Do you want to have solid tax havens and ways to reduce the taxes you pay? This book is for you! Learn how to get rich in spite of the updated 1997 tax laws. See new tax credits, year-end maneuvers, and methods for transferring and controlling your entities. Learn to structure yourself and your family for tax savings and liability protection.

Wealth 101
By Wade B. Cook

This incredible book brings you 101 strategies for wealth creation and protection that you can't afford to miss. Front to back, it is packed full of tips and tricks to supercharge your financial health. If you need to generate more cash flow, this book shows you how through several various avenues. If you are already wealthy, this is the book that will show you strategy upon strategy for decreasing your tax liability and increasing your peace of mind through liability protection.

A+
By Wade B. Cook

A+ is a collection of wisdom, thoughts, and principles of success which can help you make millions, even billions of dollars and live an A+ life. As you will see, Wade Cook consistently tries to live his life "in the second mile," to do more than asked, to be above normal.

If you want to live a successful life, you need great role models to follow. For years, Wade Cook's life has been a quest to find successful characteristics of his role models and implement them in his own life. In *A+*, Wade will encourage you to find and incorporate the most successful principles and characteristics of success in your life, too. Don't spend another day living less than an A+ life!

BUSINESS BUY THE BIBLE
By Wade B. Cook

Inspired by the Creator, the Bible truly is the authority for running the business of life. Throughout *Business Buy The Bible*, you are provided with practical advice that helps you apply God's word to your life. You'll learn how you can apply God's words to saving, spending and investing, and how you can control debt instead of being controlled by it. You'll also learn how to use God's principles in your daily business activities and prosper.

DON'T SET GOALS
By Wade B. Cook

Don't Set Goals will teach you to be a goal-getter, not just a goal-setter. You'll learn that achieving goals is the result of prioritizing and acting. *Don't Set Goals* shows you how taking action and "paying the price" is more important than simply making the decision to do something. Don't just set goals. Go out and get your goals, go where you want to go!

WADE COOK'S POWER QUOTES, VOLUME 1
By Wade B. Cook

Wade Cook's Power Quotes, Volume 1 is chock full of exciting quotes that have motivated and inspired Mr. Cook. Wade Cook continually asks his students, "To whom are you listening?" He knows that if you get your advice and inspiration from successful people, you'll become successful yourself. He compiled *Wade Cook's Power Quotes, Volume 1* to provide you with a millionaire-on-call when you need advice.

Y2K GOLD RUSH
By Wade B. Cook

As we approach the end of the millennium, newspapers and television newscasters drone on about Y2K. Computers will read the year 2000 as 1900! The issue is a definite problem, but in *Y2K Gold Rush*, Wade Cook discounts the need for this hysteria. First, businesses and individuals alike have been preparing for this problem. Secondly, and more importantly, people are now buying gold to protect themselves against all types of potential problems.

Over the last 14 years, in his financial seminars, Wade Cook has encouraged people to buy gold coins. Gold retains its value, becoming a hedge against inflation. If a need should ever arise for cash, to buy some groceries or to pay a doctor's bill, then all you have to do is go to a coin dealer and cash in. Gold coins are legal tender.

This book is about how to invest in gold. By reading *Y2K Gold Rush*, you will understand the historical importance of gold. You will learn about the ownership of gold coins and gold stocks, and the benefits of both. You will see that adding gold to your investment portfolio will diversify your assets, safeguard you and your family against catastrophe, and add excitement and profits.

Wade Cook has a positive outlook on the future and is worried about potential problems but focuses on solutions. He is preparing for the new millennium. The question is, are you?

LIVING IN COLOR
By Renae Knapp

Renae Knapp is the leading authority on the Blue Base/Yellow Base Color System and is recognized worldwide for her research and contribution to the study of color. Industries, universities, and men and women around the globe use Renae's tried and true—scientifically proven—system to achieve measurable results.

In *Living In Color*, Renae Knapp teaches you easy to understand methods which empower you to get more from your life by harnessing the power of color. In an engaging, straightforward way, Renae Knapp teaches the scientific Blue Base/Yellow Base Color System and how to achieve harmony and peace using color. You will develop a mastery of color harmony and an awareness of the amazing role color plays in every area of your life.

VIDEOS

DYNAMIC DOLLARS VIDEO
By Wade B. Cook

Wade Cook's 90 minute introduction to the basics of his Wall Street formulas and strategies. In this presentation designed especially for video, Wade explains the meter drop philosophy, Rolling Stocks, the basics of Proxy Investing, and writing Covered Calls. Perfect for anyone looking for a little basic information.

THE WALL STREET WORKSHOP™ VIDEO SERIES
By Wade B. Cook

If you can't make it to the Wall Street Workshop™ soon, get a head start with these videos. Ten albums containing 11 hours of intense instruction on Rolling Stock, options on stock split companies, writing Covered Calls, and eight other tested and proven strategies designed to help you increase the value of your investments. By learning, reviewing, and implementing the strategies taught here, you will gain the knowledge and the confidence to take control of your investments and get your money to work hard for you.

THE NEXT STEP VIDEO SERIES
By Team Wall Street

The advanced version of the Wall Street Workshop™. Full of power-packed strategies from Wade Cook, this is not a duplicate of the Wall Street Workshop™, but a very important partner. The methods taught in this seminar will supercharge the strategies taught in the Wall Street Workshop™ and teach you even more ways to make more money!

In The Next Step, you'll learn how to find the stocks to fit the formulas through technical analysis, fundamentals, home trading tools, and more.

BUILD PERPETUAL INCOME (BPI)—A VIDEOCASSETTE

Wade Cook Seminars, Inc. is proud to present Build Perpetual Income, the latest in our ever-expanding series of seminar home study courses. In this video, you will learn powerful real estate cash-flow generating techniques, such as:

- Power negotiating strategies
- Writing contracts
- Avoiding debt
- Buying and selling mortgages
- Finding and buying discount properties

CLASSES OFFERED

COOK UNIVERSITY

People enroll in Cook University for a variety of reasons. Usually they are a little discontented with where they are—their job is not working, their business is not producing the kind of income they want, or they definitely see that they need more income to prepare for a better retirement. That's where Cook University comes in. As you try to live the American Dream, in the life-style you want, we stand by ready to assist you make the dream your reality.

The backbone of the one-year program is the Money Machine concept; as applied to your business, to stock investments, or to real estate. Although there are many, many other forms of investing in real estate, there are really only three that work: the Money Machine method, buying second mortgages, and lease options. Of these three, the Money Machine stands head and shoulders above the rest.

It is difficult to explain Cook University in only a few words. It is so unique, innovative and creative that it literally stands alone. But then, what would you expect from Wade Cook? Something common and ordinary? Never! Wade and his staff always go out of their way to provide you with useful, tried-and-true strategies that create real wealth.

We are embarking on an unprecedented voyage and want you to come along. Yes, it takes commitment. Yes, it takes drive. Add to this the help you'll receive by our hand-trained experts and you will enhance your asset base and increase your bottom line.

We want to encourage a lot of people to get in the program right away. You could save thousands of dollars if you don't delay. Call right away! Class sizes are limited so each student gets personal attention.

Perpetual monthly income is waiting. We'll teach you how to achieve it. We'll show you how to make it. We'll watch over you while you're making it happen.

Cook University is designed to be an integral part of your educational life. We encourage you to call and find out more about this life-changing program. The number is 1-800-872-7411. Ask for an enrollment director and begin your millionaire-training today!

If you want to be wealthy, this is the place to be.

THE WALL STREET WORKSHOP™

Presented by Wade B. Cook and Team Wall Street

The Wall Street Workshop™ teaches you how to make incredible money in all markets. It teaches you the tried-and-true strategies that have made hundreds of people wealthy.

YOUTH WALL STREET WORKSHOP

Presented by Team Wall Street

Wade Cook has made a personal commitment to empower the youth of today with desire and knowledge to be self sufficient. Now you too can make a personal commitment to your youth by sending them to the Youth Wall Street Workshop and start your own family dynasty in the process!

Our Youth Wall Street Workshop teaches the power and money making potential of the stock market strategies of the Wall Street Workshop™. The pace is geared to the students, with more time devoted to vocabulary, principles and concepts that may be new to them.

Your children and grandchildren can learn these easy to understand strategies and get that "head start" in life!

If you're considering the Wall Street Workshop™ for the first time, take advantage of our free Youth Wall Street Workshop promotion and bring a son, daughter, or grandchild with you (ages 13 to 18, student, living at home).

Help make your children financially secure in the future by giving them the helping hand in life we all wish we had received.

FINANCIAL CLINIC

Presented by Wade Cook and Team Wall Street

People from all over are making money, lots of money, in the stock market using the proven bread and butter strategies taught by Wade Cook. Is trading in the stock market for you?

Please accept our invitation to come hear for yourself the amazing money-making strategies we teach. Our Financial Clinic is designed to help you understand how you can learn these proven stock market strategies. In three short hours you will be introduced to some of the 11 proven strategies we teach at our Wall Street Workshop™. Discover for yourself how they work and how you can use them in your life to get the things you want for you and your family. Come to this introductory event and see what we have to offer. Then make the decision yourself!

THE NEXT STEP WORKSHOP
Presented by Wade B. Cook and Team Wall Street

An Advanced Wall Street Workshop designed to help those ready to take their trading to the next level and treat it as a business. This seminar is open only to graduates of the Wall Street Workshop™.

S.O.A.R. (SUPERCHARGING OTHERWISE AVERAGE RETURNS)
Presented by Bob Eldridge

This one-day workshop begins by teaching you some basic trading strategies using a "hands-on" approach. You will be amazed at how easy it is to apply these strategies to the 30 Dow Jones Industrial Average stocks. Using these strategies, Bob Eldridge was able to resign from his job as an air traffic control specialist and begin speaking full-time after only a few months of trading!

THE ONE-MINUTE COMMUTE (TRADING AT HOME)
Presented by Keven Hart

This one-day clinic will take you from being a semi-active investor to trading on a daily basis, giving you the freedom to dictate your own schedule and move forward on your own pre-determined timeline. Trade from your home and stay close to your family. This condensed training will get you where you want to go by helping you practice trading as a business, showing you which resources produce wealth through crucial and timely information, selecting appropriate strategies, qualifying your trades and helping you time both entries and exits.

THE DAY TRADER
Presented by Mike Coval

The Day Trader will teach you how to locate and profit on a daily basis from charts, news, and trends. You will also learn how outside indicators can and will influence a market. Learn how to find the hottest stocks in the hottest sectors and find out a stock's movement before the market opens. With this action-packed workshop, you will have the opportunity to find fast-moving stocks profiting in just minutes. At the end of each day you can sit back and count your profits, then start tomorrow all over again!

EXECUTIVE RETREAT
Presented by Wade B. Cook and Team Wall Street

Created especially for the individuals already owning or planning to establish Nevada Corporations, the Executive Retreat is a unique opportunity for corporate executives to participate in workshops geared toward streamlining operations and maximizing efficiency.

WEALTH INSTITUTE

Presented by Wade B. Cook and Team Wall Street

This three-day workshop defines the art of asset protection and entity planning. During these three days we will discuss, in depth and detail, the six domestic entities which will protect you from lawsuits, taxes, or other financial losses, and help you retire rich.

REAL ESTATE WORKSHOP

Presented by Wade B. Cook and Team Main Street

The Real Estate Workshop teaches you how to build perpetual income for life, without going to work. Some of the topics include buying and selling paper, finding discounted properties, generating long-term monthly cash flow, and controlling properties without owning them.

REAL ESTATE BOOTCAMP

Presented by Wade B. Cook and Team Main Street

This three to four day bootcamp is truly a roll-up-your-sleeves and do-the-deals event. You will be learning how to locate the bargains, negotiate strategies, and find wholesale properties (pre-foreclosures). You will also visit a title company, look at properties and learn some new and fun selling strategies.

BUSINESS ENTITY SKILLS TRAINING (BEST)

Presented by Wade B. Cook and Team Wall Street

Learn about the six powerful entities you can use to protect your wealth and your family. Learn the secrets of asset protection, eliminate your fear of litigation, and minimize your taxes.

ASSORTED RESOURCES

WEALTH INFORMATION NETWORK™ (W.I.N.™)

This subscription Internet service provides you with the latest financial formulas and updated entity structuring strategies. New, timely information is entered Monday through Friday, sometimes four or five times a day. Wade Cook and his Team Wall Street staff write for W.I.N.™, giving you updates on their own current stock plays, companies who announced earnings, companies who announced stock splits, and the latest trends in the market.

W.I.N.™ is also divided into categories according to specific strategies and contains archives of all their trades so you can view their history. If you are just getting started in the stock market, this is a great way to follow people who are experiencing above-average returns. If you are experienced already, it's the way to confirm your feelings and research with others who are generating wealth through the stock market.

IQ PAGER™

This is a system that beeps you as events and announcements are made on Wall Street. With IQ Pager™, you'll receive information about events like major stock split announcements, earnings surprises, important mergers and acquisitions, judgments or court decisions involving big companies, important bankruptcy announcements, big winners and losers, and disasters. If you're getting your financial information from the evening news, you're getting it too late. The key to the stock market is timing. Especially when you're trading in options, you need up-to-the-minute (or second) information. You cannot afford to sit at a computer all day looking for news or wait for your broker to call. IQ Pager™ is the ideal partner to the Wealth Information Network™ (W.I.N.™).

THE INCORPORATION HANDBOOK
By Wade B. Cook

Incorporation made easy! This handbook tells you who, why, and, most importantly, how to incorporate. Included are samples of the forms you will use when you incorporate, as well as a step-by-step guide from the experts.

LEGAL FORMS
By Wade B. Cook

This collection of pertinent forms contains numerous legal forms used in real estate transactions. These forms were selected by experienced investors, but are not intended to replace the advice of an attorney. However, they will provide essential forms for you to follow in your personal investing.

RECORD KEEPING SYSTEM
By Wade B. Cook

A complete record keeping system for organizing all of the information on each of your properties. This system keeps track of everything from insurance policies to equity growth. You will know at a glance exactly where you stand with your investment properties and you will sleep better at night.

TRAVEL AGENT INFORMATION
By John Childers and Wade Cook

The only sensible solution for the frequent traveler. This kit includes all of the information and training you need to be an outside travel agent for a stable company. There are no hassles, no requirements, no forms or restrictions, just all the benefits of traveling for substantially less every time.

EXPLANATIONS NEWSLETTER

In the wild and crazy stock market game, *EXPLANATIONS NEWSLETTER* will keep you on your toes! Every month you'll receive coaching, instruction and encouragement with engaging articles designed to bring your trading skills to a higher level. Learn new twists on Wade Cook's 11 basic strategies, find out about beneficial research tools, read reviews on the latest investment products and services, and get detailed answers to your trading questions. With *EXPLANATIONS*, you'll learn to be your own best asset in the stock market game and stay on track to a rapidly growing portfolio! Continue your education as an investor and subscribe today!

APPENDIX 3
Fraction To Decimal Conversion

Fraction		Decimal	Fraction		Decimal
$1/32$	. . . .	.03125	$17/32$	. . . .	.53125
$1/16$	. . . .	.0625	$9/16$	. . . .	.5625
$3/32$	. . . .	.09375	$19/32$	. . . .	.59375
$1/8$	. . . .	.125	$5/8$	. . . .	.625
$5/32$	. . . .	.15625	$21/32$	. . . .	.65625
$3/16$	. . . .	.1875	$11/16$	. . . .	.6875
$7/32$	. . . .	.21875	$23/32$	. . . .	.71875
$1/4$	. . . .	.25	$3/4$	. . . .	.75
$9/32$	. . . .	.28125	$25/32$	. . . .	.78125
$5/16$	. . . .	.3125	$13/16$	. . . .	.8125
$11/32$	. . . .	.34375	$27/32$	. . . .	.84375
$3/8$	. . . .	.375	$7/8$	. . . .	.875
$13/32$	. . . .	.40625	$29/32$	. . . .	.90625
$7/16$	. . . .	.4375	$15/16$	. . . .	.9375
$15/32$	. . . .	.46875	$31/32$	. . . .	.96875
$1/2$	. . . .	.5			

GLOSSARY

Ask - The current price for which a security may be bought (purchased).

Balance of Power™ - A technical indicator developed by Worden Brothers, which shows patterns of systematic buying and selling by informed buyers.

Bid - The current price at which a stock is selling.

Breakout - This term is shown on the graph when the stock price either goes above the resistance level or goes below the support level (also called breakdown) when it breaks out of its current pattern or trend.

Call - An option contract giving the owner the right (not the obligation) to buy 100 shares of stock at a strike price on or before the expiration date.

Call spread - The result of an investor buying a call on a particular security and writing a call with a different expiration date, different exercise price, or both, on the same security.

Cover - Stock purchased to offset a short position.

Covered call writer - An investor who writes a call and owns some other asset that guarantees the ability to perform if the call is exercised.

Day order - A limit order with a specific duration of one day.

Fundamental Analysis (or fundamentals) - The study of a company's financial reports, marketing, management, and overall business characteristics as a means of determining the value of the stock.

Gaps - Gaps show on a chart when the stock's price either rises dramatically in a short time period or loses value in a short time. This creates a physical gap or space in between opening and closing prices.

LEAPS® (Long-term Equity Anticipation Securities) - an option with a long-term expiration date.

Long - Owning the security on which an option is written.

Margin - Effectively, a loan from the broker, allowing the investor to purchase securities of a greater value than actual cash available in the account.

Margin account - An account in which a brokerage firm lends a client part of the purchase price of securities.

Margin calls - A demand for a client to deposit money or securities when a purchase is made in excess of the value of a margin account.

Market order - An order to buy or sell a stock or option at the current market price.

Market value - The price at which an investor will buy or sell each share of common stock or each bond at a given time.

MoneyStream™ (also Cumulative MoneyStream™ or CMS) - A technical tool developed by Worden Brothers as a cumulative price/volume indicator. Upward sloping regression lines show patterns in buying and selling of stock.

Moving Average - An average that moves forward with time, dropping earlier components as later ones are added. This is an analytical tool, which smooths out the fluctuations of a stock chart.

News - Referring to the volatility of the movement of a particular stock being affected by news, not by any intrinsic value to the company.

Option - The right to buy (or sell) a specified amount of a security (stocks, bonds, futures contracts, et cetera) at a specified price on or before a specific date (American style options).

Paper trade (see Simutrade) - A trade recorded and tracked, but not using actual funds in a brokerage account. These are done as a means of learning and testing a strategy.

Put - An option contract that gives the owner the right to sell a specified number of shares of stock at a specified price on or before a specific date.

Put spread - An investment in which an investor purchases one put on a particular stock and sells another put on the same stock but with a different expiration date, exercise price, or both.

Range rider - A stock that has highs and lows on its price range and gradually rises to a high range over a period of time.

Resistance - The upper level of a stock's trading range at which a stock's price appears to be limited in upward movement (see Support).

Rolling options - A strategy of buying calls or puts on a Rolling Stock.

Rolling stocks - A stock that fluctuates between its high and low price points for long periods of time and whose history makes it seem to be predictable.

Short - A condition resulting from selling an option and not owning the related securities.

Simutrade - A trade recorded and tracked, but not using actual funds in a brokerage account. Traders Simutrade as a means of learning and testing a strategy.

Spread - 1) Consisting of being a buyer and seller of the same type of option with the options having different exercise prices and/or expiration dates. 2) The difference between the bid and ask for a stock or option.

Stochastics - A technical indicator showing where the price of a stock is trading in a given range.

Stock split - A reduction in the par value of stock caused by the issuance of additional stock.

Stop order - A limit order placed to protect account value from a significant decline in the price of a stock.

Strike price - The price at which the underlying security will be sold if the option buyer exercises his/her rights in the contract.

Support - The lower level of a stock's trading range at which there appears to be a limit on further price declines (see Resistance).

Technical analysis (or technicals) - The study of stock charts indicators like market sentiment, price, trading, and volume patterns to determine future price movements.

Ticker symbol - A trading symbol used by a company to identify it on a stock exchange.

Trendline - The long-term direction of a stock's movement as plotted on a chart.

Volatile - When speaking of the stock market and of stocks or securities, this is when the market tends to vary often and wildly in prices.

ABOUT THE AUTHOR

David Hebert Sr, grew up in San Diego, California. Joining the military at 17, he served eight years in the air force as a jet mechanic and aircraft mechanic instructor. After the military, he worked in Boeing's 747 flight test program.

He later spent 25 years working in the Railroad industry, eventually starting his own business manufacturing locomotive and marine diesel engine components in 1978. Ten years later, his company was sold after reaching 10 million in sales. He traveled extensively throughout the United States, South America and Mexico conducting workshops in relation to diesel engine maintenance and railroad related subjects. He took over as Chief Operating Officer of the North Coast Railroad in 1993.

He has studied electrical engineering and holds a degree in Business and Industrial Marketing. He also has a commercial pilots license, and is a certified locomotive engineer.

David Hebert has been trading in the stock market since 1986 and has been a serious investor since 1996.

David currently resides in Lake Tapps, Washington with his wife of 36 years, Diana. He has 6 children, and 15 grandchildren. He is active in his church and enjoys boating and golfing.